Live
Love
Laugh

Carolyn
Coppola

Published by CC Press Inc.

ISBN# 97809881746-1-0

Copyright
7/14/2012 Library of Congress Registration Number:
TXu001818924
Carolyn Susan Coppola

www.CarolynCoppola.com

Back cover photo by Cristen Farrel
www.CristenFarrel.com

For Grace

You really are amazing...

CONTENTS

THERE IS NO DENYING THAT MOTHERHOOD IS A TOUGH JOB. There are times when I fully rely on my sense of humor just to get through the day. Even though in "Minivans, Meltdowns and Merlot", I may portray myself as one of the most frazzled mom's of all time, it's a job that I wouldn't trade for anything in the world! While there are a great many challenges that come with the enormous responsibility of raising children, there are just as many rewards—if not more. Above all else, I consider motherhood a gift from God, a true miracle and I feel overwhelmingly blessed to be a mom!

As difficult as I may have found some days, unfortunately, there are many mothers out there who have far greater struggles than I could possibly imagine. There are families who must garner all of their strength as their children fight illnesses no child should ever have to face. My husband's younger sister, Kathy, lost her battle against cancer when she was thirteen. In her honor, a percentage of every copy of "Minivans, Meltdowns and Merlot" sold will be donated to Children's Hospital in Boston.

Writing "Minivans, Meltdowns & Merlot" was an amazing journey and a dream come true. There were many special people along the way that I am deeply grateful for. First and foremost, thank you to my husband John. I can honestly say that this book would never have made it to print if not for your constant encouragement, love and unwavering support. I love you with all my heart and soul as well as our life of love and laughter together. To my children, who have taught me the pure joy of unconditional love, thank you for being the best kids a mother could ever ask for! You make me proud every single day!

To my parents, sister, friends and family: I am honored to be a part of this incredible circle of love. To Melissa Ouellette, thank you for the inspiration you have given me, the hilarious material pulled directly out of your own adventures in motherhood and for all of the laughs we've shared along the way.

Deep gratitude to all of the moms in my life, especially, Leigh Tuccolo, Lynn Giordano, Nancy LaCourse and Dalyne Villeneuve, for helping to shape this book by sharing your own tales of motherhood and being there to help keep me afloat in this sea of Motherhood. I couldn't have survived this far without you! I am truly thankful for all of the years of listening, laughing, sharing, and advising. To Shell, Sherry, Sue and Sandy, Thank you for lifting me up and lighting the way!

And last but certainly not least to Sarah Teres, for being the first person to ever encourage me to put my stories down on paper. For being the most brilliant and fantastic Editor any writer could ever hope to work with. For helping me to create a story in the way it was meant to be, by taking my short stories and weaving them all together in only a way that you could. For your wisdom and insight and most of all for your willingness to share your god given gifts and talents with me through taking on this project. There are no coincidences in life, and I will always be grateful that we were brought together again. Thank you from the bottom of my heart!

Many names in this book have been changed to protect the privacy of friends and family.

Minivans, Meltdowns and Merlot

WEIRD THINGS HAVE ALWAYS HAPPENED TO CHRISSY and her third pregnancy was no exception. For some reason, her body made an abundant quantity of amniotic fluid. Where most pregnant women have just enough amniotic fluid to nourish and protect their baby, Chrissy had enough fluid for three babies. So although she only had *one* baby in her womb, she was carrying the equivalent weight of triplets.

That fateful day while shopping for a new car, my poor friend waddled onto the lot feeling like an elephant laboring in the jungle. Her feet were swollen like sausages and her blonde hair frizzed from the thick, muggy air.

Shopping for a car was the *last* thing on her mind that day and she knew that no matter what, it would be an impossible task to try to squeeze her gigantic belly into any of the cars on the lot. She couldn't fathom how she would test drive any vehicle in her condition. Despite the fact that Chrissy and her triplet-equivalent belly weren't going to test drive anything—even a Humvee, she walked right past the minivans and confidently strolled over toward the Jeep line up. She was determined to stand her ground, even if it meant giving birth right there on the steaming hot pavement. It was no easy feat but somehow, with great effort (and more than a little sweat) as she sashayed over to the Jeeps, she yelled to get her husband's attention.

"Hey Mike! Come here and check *this* out! I absolutely love it! I can really see myself and the three kids cruising around in this—what do you think?" she asked, pointing to a sparkling silver Jeep Cherokee. "Well, yes it's beautiful honey," said Mike, "but it's out of our price range and it's not really practical," he stressed, as he pushed her back toward the row of minivans.

"Why are we going this way?" she whimpered. "I'd rather ride the public bus than drive a minivan! What is wrong with you?" she cried. Her husband, losing patience but knowing he was dealing with nine months of pregnancy hormones said, "Would you get over it? You're a mom now and you're about to have baby #3, it's time to face the facts: we're getting a Minivan. Come along now let's go and check out that white one over there. It looks like a beauty."

"You know I hate white!" she said. "I didn't even wear it on our wedding day! And to tell you the truth, I hate all of these colors. There isn't one on this lot that I would be happy with—this is a nightmare!" she uttered in vain.

It was obvious that the salesman could sense the tension and with a painted on grin he said, "Now, don't worry, I've got plenty more out back. I'm sure I can find something that will make you both very happy." Chrissy protested with a pout, "Why should you make him happy? He's not the one who has to drive it. He's not the one throwing his manhood out the window.

I'm the one who has to be seen in it! Plus I know, all too well, the fury that will go on inside that thing. I can guarantee you, it's not gonna be pretty. Big Bird cups will be chucked at my head, mini Nike's will be flying out the window, my hair will be standing on edge and I will be broken down to the point of tears on many occasions. If *I* am the one dealing with all of that, then at least I should be able to drive something that I like."

She started to feel her giant belly tighten and contract, as Mr. "Let's Make a Deal" walked away. She tried to remember her breathing exercises as she inhaled a deep breath and slowly exhaled. "Breathe in, breathe out, isn't that what they taught me in birthing classes? Visualize something relaxing—focus— get my mind off the pain. Yeah, that's it...focus on something positive. Think nice, happy, thoughts." She smiled, imagining herself lunging at that jerk with the patronizing grin and the obvious black toupee. As her uterus tightened, she envisioned her hands tightening into a noose around his neck. She saw herself squeezing that scrawny little neck and while giving birth to a new life, she'd choke the old life right out of him.

Chrissy couldn't believe what a nerve he had! To think a woman like her would want to drive off in one of his pathetic minivans. Sweat poured off her forehead, as she willed the growing agony in her belly to go away. Her abdomen cramped again as he came back, waltzing around the corner sporting a huge, victorious and obnoxious smile. His smug attitude conveyed that behind door #2, (the one she clearly had not chosen) was a shiny new minivan...in Burgundy. Grimacing in obvious physical pain, she threw her arms in the air and almost wept as she admitted, "Well, I guess it *is* a pretty color." She signed the purchase agreement and along with it, signed away all hopes and dreams of being anything less than a minivan mama.

As sad as Chrissy's story may be, it's not unique. Four out of Five in our circle of mom friends now drive a Minivan. Sooner or later, you must face the inevitable and cave in to the company car that comes with the job of motherhood. I'm the odd woman out because I haven't found myself behind the wheel of one...yet.

Although, I did come a little too close for comfort one day when my husband's old Chevy Blazer broke down for the millionth time and he went to the dealership to attempt to put another Band-Aid on it.

However, the Blazer's last life had expired and he got pissed enough to drive off the lot with a new...GMC Envoy. He didn't have a whole lot of choice because, with no car, he had to buy something right then and there or call "Family Cab" for a ride home.

As it happened, he got a good deal on a demo model of the Envoy with a third row of seats. Since we had just had another baby, he knew the extra row of seats would be vital.

We never so much as had a discussion about a new car as he simply pulled into the driveway with it. I was lucky. I suppose it could have just as easily been a brand new burgundy minivan making a grand entrance into my driveway that day.

The GMC Envoy *technically* isn't considered a minivan, even though it really does look and act a lot like one. More than a few times people have referred to the Envoy as a van and I suddenly find myself becoming defensive. I correct them by saying something like, "Oh that's not a minivan, it's an Envoy." They look at me like I'm in denial and shake their head as if to say, "Whatever lady! If the shoe fits, wear it."

Well, I'll admit I've gotten more comfortable wearing those shoes. Either that or I simply don't have time to worry about what people think I'm driving anymore. I guess when it comes right down to it, if you pack any vehicle full of kids with their arms flailing, French Fries flying, drinks spilling, does it really make that much of a difference what *kind* of vehicle it actually is? I've come to realize that it's essential to have a car big enough to fit kids and all the paraphernalia that comes along with them. It just goes with the territory.

One of the best features of having a car this size is the "way back", as we like to call it. It's the perfect solution when you've got a kid who needs to be stored far away from the rest of the family. Since it's not legal or socially acceptable to tie your tantruming kid to the roof, at least you have a viable option with the third row seating.

Whoever designed this gets an A+ for research. Maybe they did a test drive with a few bratty kids in the design model. Maybe they had a terrible two-year-old who didn't like his shoes and socks or was particularly skilled at throwing a bottle full of milk at his big brother. They would have found out soon enough that, more than anything else, the third row seat's best feature is for banishing unruly children. I worship my "way back". Kids and meltdowns are synonymous and the further away from me they are when they do it, the better.

I still remember our first "girl's night out" in my friend Jenn's minivan. We had all been so busy having babies, that all of our birthdays came and went without notice. We decided to get together and have a long overdue night out. Anyone who saw us that night probably thought we'd been locked away from civilization for months. In a way, we had been. Locked away somewhere on a remote island filled with jars of baby food, cheerios, dirty diapers, Mr. Noodle, and formerly white onesies.

We couldn't break out of those mommy straight jackets fast enough and were itching to bust out and get into our own kid-free mischief. I couldn't help but imagine which one of us might end up banished to the "way back" that night.

Our friend Jenn, God bless her, kindly offered to be the Designated Driver that night. She has always been a lightweight anyway. She never drinks more than one Margarita and even with that, she always leaves her glass half full. I can't stand to see people waste good booze and it would always leave me wondering if I could somehow guzzle the rest of her drink without appearing to be a raging alcoholic.

Contrary to my having previously thought that everyone hates their minivans, Jenn didn't seem all that depressed when she announced to us all that she just bought one. She has the best sense of humor and she laughed when she said, "Let's go—it's girls night out in the minivan!" Nobody cared how we got to the restaurant, only that we got there. Once we had a bottle of Merlot sitting on the table, everything was suddenly right with the world.

We happily toasted to our temporary freedom, "Here's to being unsaddled tonight! Here's to not having to spell out the bad words! Here's to surviving the mayhem of motherhood!" And finally, as we clinked our glasses one last time, Jenn said, "And here's to all of us—the minivan mamas!"

I was so happy to be there, caught up in the moment of great friends and good wine, that for once, I didn't even bother to explain that my Envoy *technically* wasn't really...a minivan.

Neighborhood Search Party

WHEN MY HUSBAND AND I FIRST WERE MARRIED, we lived in a two family home in a quiet neighborhood. The houses were close together and we didn't have much of a yard but at the time, it was perfect for us. The income from the apartment upstairs helped pay the rent and since the middle school was right around the corner, it was convenient for my stepchildren to be able to walk home after school. It would have been even more perfect if not for Rose—the old lady next door. I could never forget that woman even if I tried.

One of her favorite past times was to spy on us through her kitchen window. She probably didn't have anything better to do and I would bet if I was someone like her and somebody like me lived next door, I'd probably spy on me too. I can still remember the way that she would strategically pull back her little white curtains with a hair clip, which was just enough to give her a perfect view.

We had lived there for several years when I discovered she had been spying on us. For some reason, even though the houses were practically connected, it never occurred to me that she would do such a thing. The first time I realized just how much she *actually* knew about what was going on in our home happened to be when she casually mentioned she'd seen my son painting while he was naked. She asked me why I was allowing my son to paint in his birthday suit.

I was speechless when I heard the words coming out of her mouth. I couldn't believe that she was able to see that clearly into my house, especially through my kitchen window. God knows my kitchen windows were never the shiniest windows on the block but even then I thought, "What? Oh come on! I mean, really?" She must have had a pair of binoculars to see something so specific, especially at her age.

I will admit that, yes, my kid did love to paint and yes, I did let him do it while he was naked. I figured, why not let him paint naked? Believe me, it was a whole lot easier than trying to get the paint out of his clothes. I could just throw him into the tub when he was done and it was easy as could be with no extra laundry! I don't know what upset me more, that she was admitting to spying on us or that she had the nerve to question my parenting.

Later that night I thought about what Rose had said, wondering how she could see so much of what was going on in our home. I was a bit disturbed when I remembered all of the times I had been in the kitchen ironing my clothes, while only wearing underwear and bra. Worse still was I'd done that more than a few times when I was nine months pregnant and about to burst. She must have *really* gotten an eyeful those last few weeks of my pregnancy!

Of course I'd heard about nosey neighbors before, who

hasn't? But for me, Rose really took the cake. I must admit though, that despite her daily viewing of my family reality show, I actually did like the woman. She was thoughtful as well as kind and on many occasions, I really did enjoy our conversations in the back yard. She was a widow and I knew she was lonely, so I found it in my heart to forgive her chronic nosiness. Either that, or I was simply grateful that my bedroom was on the *other* side of the house.

One afternoon, I took my two-year-old son outside to play on the swings in our backyard. He was happily climbing up and down the ladder on the slide when Rose called me over to her side of the yard. She wanted to give me some parenting magazines that she'd been saving for me. I didn't bother to question why a seventy plus year old woman would even *have* parenting magazines.

Thinking back on it now, maybe it was because her only child still lived with her and he was fifty years old. Who knows? Maybe she was looking for tips on what she did wrong? Or how to get him to move out? I suppose it's also possible that she was hoping I'd take some parenting points on how to put my kid in a smock while playing Picasso. She handed me the old magazines and I thanked her as I turned around to check on my son.

My heart skipped a beat when I realized that he wasn't there. It was like he had disappeared into thin air. I immediately turned to Rose and said, "Oh my god Rose! Where did he go?" She just smiled and said, "Oh don't worry dear, I never took my eyes off of him, not for a second. He's right there in the garage." I breathed a little easier as I ran into the garage to find him but he was nowhere to be found. No matter how many times I looked, I couldn't find him. It was as though he had just...vanished.

Inside the garage was a lot of old furniture covered by tarps, so of course I lifted and pulled all of the tarps away but even after that, Tommy was nowhere to be found. My heart sank as I noticed a ladder going up to the garage ceiling. "Why is there a ladder going up to the ceiling?" I thought to myself, while making a mental note to kill my husband. I looked up with pure fear as I saw at the top of the ladder there were only a few planks running each way across the ceiling beams.

This was definitely my worst nightmare. To think, even for a minute, that my two-year-old had climbed up there was enough to stop me from breathing. I frantically climbed the ladder as fast as I could and peered around the entire area. Much to my relief, there was no sign of my baby. I climbed down and ran back outside. I begged Rose three more times to tell me where he could be. She swore up and down that he never left the garage. I took into account that she was an expert at spying and was probably right, so I tore the garage apart and moved everything that I could physically move. I could not find my child no matter where I looked.

I was all too familiar with the speed in which a two-year-old can move. I knew how easily he would have been able to slip out of the yard in seconds flat, so I immediately ran behind the garage. The back of my house led to another neighbor's yard and he could have gotten to the road from there. Although our house was on a side street, it was only three houses in and away from a main road. My heart was racing a mile a minute and I felt like my throat was beginning to close up as I ran around my neighborhood like a maniac. I was telling anybody who would listen that my little boy was missing. People started flocking from all around the area and within minutes, formed a neighborhood search party.

There were people on bikes looking everywhere, while children and adults alike were screaming his name up and down the road. By that time, I was in full-blown panic mode. When somebody asked me to describe what my son was wearing, I couldn't think straight and felt like my entire mind and body were paralyzed with fear. I was running around frantically but as I tried to scream his name, no words would come out.

In my hysteria, I snagged my pants on a fence and ripped a giant hole right in the crotch as I lurched over it. For a split second, I was stuck on that fence and was afraid I wouldn't be able to clear it. I am not the most athletic person to begin with, so jumping fences wasn't really something I've ever been skilled at. I started running down the road parallel to mine when I heard the most glorious three words I'd ever heard in my entire life. From my own back yard, someone yelled, "I've got him!" I clumsily climbed back over the fence and ran back home, sobbing with relief.

Although my tears were flowing, I still couldn't utter any words. I was shaking all over as I listened to that man tell everybody that he had found my little boy on the plywood planks up on the ceiling of the garage. Tommy had indeed climbed that ladder and had hidden underneath a tarp after all.

Oh stupid, stupid, me! I knew his favorite game was hide and seek but still, it didn't make any rational sense how I could have missed him when I had searched up there. I felt like the worst mother in the world. How could he have been up there and I didn't notice? I had checked and double, even triple, checked. I climbed that ladder to the top and looked everywhere. I had even shouted his name. No matter how hard I tried, I just couldn't comprehend how I wasn't able to find him.

I was dumbfounded when I asked the man who found Tommy how he knew he was up there. He said it was the only thing that made sense because Rose was so adamant that Tommy had never left that garage. He was so calm, cool and collected while he said it. While I, on the other hand, wouldn't know the first thing about staying calm in a crisis. At the time I thought, "Well I guess this is what happens when you *don't* panic."

The man who found Tommy told me that when he climbed the ladder and called out his name, Tommy answered, "I'm up here hiding on mommy." He did admit that once he saw how dangerous the situation was, he had started to shake in his boots as much as I had. He told me that he was petrified to carry Tommy back down the ladder and couldn't believe my son was up there either.

I still have trouble wrapping my brain around the whole thing even after so much time has passed. Tommy had to have heard all of those people calling his name. He must have thought he was the best hide and seek player going. And in a way, on that day, he was.

To this day, every time I picture those planks, it gives me chills. To think if he had crawled just a few feet in any direction, he would have plunged twelve feet down to a cement floor.

When the danger had passed, I took my beloved baby in my arms and hugged him as tight as I could. The entire neighborhood search party gathered around clapping in gratitude to the man who had saved my son. I carried Tommy into the house and sat him down on the kitchen floor while I poured myself a beer. I think I guzzled the entire glass in under a minute. I looked at the clock and saw it wasn't even noon yet but after everything that had happened, screw the rules! Noon or not, I was going to have the damn beer!

There are many moments when I wonder how I survived my son's early childhood or at least came through it relatively unscathed. Sometimes I just marvel at our good fortune, because so many of Tommy's toddler years consisted of just making sure he survived an entire day in one piece.

And for the life of me, I don't know how I made it through that time in his life—let alone how *he* did.

Footloose at the Farm

MY FRIEND DEE LIVES ON A FARM. She married a man who grew up on a farm and loved it so much he decided there was no other place he'd rather live. He worked out a deal with his dad and scored himself a beautiful piece of the family acreage. Although an engineer by trade, farming is in his blood. Most nights and weekends he can be seen on his tractor tilling the land.

I've known Dee since High School. She's one of those "perfect" people you would totally hate, except that you love them and they are one of your best friends.

Dee is absolutely gorgeous. She's a natural redhead and a great dancer who has always been able to turn more than a few heads. Although I'd always pictured her being more of a city girl, I wasn't at all surprised when she moved to the farm. I knew how much she loved her husband and respected his desire to have children and raise them on the family property.

Ever since I can remember, Dee has always loved to dance. When we were in high school, I'd show up at her house after school only to find her upstairs in her room with music blasting. Her red hair would be flying, up, down, side to side, while her arms and feet were moving wildly in sync with the beat. This was the passion that led her to meet her husband at a country western bar called "The White Buffalo". They were probably two stepping to a Brad Paisley song when they met and fell in love.

It's scary sometimes how everything changes once you fall in love and get married. And even more so once you have kids. There's not much time for dancing after you become a mom. However, dancing is exactly what Dee was doing on the day she almost got arrested.

As I said about Dee, if you didn't love her, you would hate her. She popped out two kids and still looks hot in a bikini. As if that wasn't enough to envy, you should see her eat! I can't tell you how many times I've had dinner with her, watched her pile a mountain of food on her plate and wolf it down. And mind you, that's just her *first* helping. She always goes back for more.

I've heard a few people say she stays so skinny because she chases after kids all day. I am here to tell you, that is a crock. I don't exactly lounge around on the couch all day with my feet up. I run around after two kids too but I'd never be as skinny as she is even if I added a few extra laps to my "running around after kids all day." Now that I think about it, I haven't been her size since I was probably six years old. I'm sick of hearing it's all about her "metabolism" too. One of the world's worst injustices is that some people can eat an 18-wheeler full of Frito's and not gain an ounce, while others can squint at a cookie with one eye open and gain a pound.

She still looks exactly the same as the day we graduated from high school. With her slim figure and long, gorgeous red hair she gets *a lot* of attention.

Just take a trip down to the local butcher with her someday and watch the young boys behind the counter stumble over themselves to serve her. I've never seen anyone else get a fillet mignon so cheap.

Her only physical flaw, as far as I can see, is the stress vein on her forehead. But even when it comes to her stress vein, she finds a way to make it sexy. Julia Roberts has the same kind of stress vein and when Julia's hair is red, they could be sisters. I tease her about her stress vein and call her "Julia" all the time.

One might secretly hope that because she looks so good (even after having kids), can eat whatever she wants and stay skinny that she'd be a rotten mom. Sorry to say so but that isn't true. She's a super mom. She picks fresh fruits and veggies from her own garden and feeds her children local, organic, all natural everything. She claims you can even drink her bug spray. While other kids are glued to the "magnet", as she calls it, watching endless hours of TV, her boys are outside in the fresh air. Sure, they watch TV as well but only for thirty minutes a day and what they watch is all educational programming. She keeps a list of which shows are appropriate and which ones are not. One day when she came over, my kids were watching "Sponge Bob" and she was quick to point out that unfortunately, it was one of the shows that hadn't made the "appropriate" list.

She's very organized, conscientious and she's got it all together most of the time. So imagine my surprise when she'd confessed over lunch one day that she had almost been arrested for child neglect and reckless abandonment.

Her boys are polar opposites. The oldest follows all the rules, while the little one lives to break them. I suspected her trouble may have resulted from something that her youngest boy, the little rebel, may have been involved in. Who would have thought it was actually her husband's fault? Well, it was mostly his fault.

When she told me she had nearly been arrested, I would have been less shocked if she had told me she was stripping at the local "gentlemen's club" to make ends meet. I was sitting at her kitchen table wide eyed with disbelief. "Okay, you'd better pour me a glass of wine for this one." I said.

She explained that it had all started one morning when her husband, Jack, was heading out to hay the fields. As one might imagine, the work on a farm is plenty and often times takes him almost all day to finish. He likes to make it seem horrible and labor intensive but she knows he can hardly wait to get out of the house and can't disappear outside fast enough. Ah, if only they could do a job swap once in awhile! Wouldn't that be nice? Maybe it's just me, but there's definitely something about riding around on a tractor, with the wind blowing in your hair, that just seems so much more appealing than being on your hands and knees scrubbing the kitchen floor.

The day Dee was almost arrested started out like any other sunny Saturday morning. Jack went out the kitchen door just after breakfast and their youngest boy, Garrett happily tagged along after him. Every so often Jack takes one of the boys with him to relieve some of the burden from his wife's shoulders. Since Garrett was the wild child, it was always welcomed when he was occupied and out of her hair. As much work as there is to do on a farm outside, there is always a lot to do inside as well. Dishes, dusting, laundry, scrubbing, cooking—the list is daunting.

Unlike a lot of other jobs, on a farm there is no time to procrastinate and Dee knew she had to get everything done if there was any hope of getting outside to tend to her garden.

It always seems that cleaning gets done quicker with some music playing, so Dee turned on the radio. In what felt like a matter of minutes after the music started, the dishes were washed, the dusting was done and she continued on to the laundry. When one of her favorite songs came on she couldn't resist indulging herself. She started dancing furiously around her kitchen. She relaxed knowing that her wild child was hanging out with dad, while her quiet child was in the living room working on a puzzle. She was making fairly decent progress and was pleased to see that she was half way through her work for the day and it wasn't even midday yet.

Apparently, the music was cranked loudly enough that she didn't hear the doorbell ringing or the dog barking. According to Dee, all she remembered was looking up into the faces of two cops standing in her kitchen doorway. She said, "Can't you just picture it? The radio blaring, while I'm spinning around my kitchen in my short shorts—I don't even know *how* long they had been watching me!" I shook my head and said, "Oh my god! I would have died!" She said, "Oh yeah. And did I mention that I wasn't wearing a bra?" With a slight giggle I answered, "No you didn't mention that! So, what did you do?" She shrugged her shoulders and added, "Well, what else could I do? I ran over to the radio, turned it off and tried my best to hide my boobs."

Still wondering where the cops came from in the first place, she innocently asked, "How can I help you officers?" The younger cop who Dee mentioned had dark, wavy hair and bright blue eyes looked her up and down and said, "Did you lose something Ma'am?" She indignantly sniped. "Can you believe

he called me Ma'am? Ewww! When did *I* become a Ma'am?"
She let the insult go and answered him with, "Well, no, not that
I know of, why do you ask"? While her mouth spoke one thing,
her mind entertained another, "Well, yes Mr. Hot Cop, I have
lost something—my mind. But that was a long time ago after
my first son was born." A few seconds later Dee saw that the
older officer behind "Mr. Hot Cop" had her two year old by the
hand and immediately she knew what she'd "lost".

Frantically, Dee ran to her child and scooped him up. She
was hugging him while crying, "How on Earth did this happen?
Wherever did you find my son and where is my irresponsible
husband?" The Officers explained that they had found Garrett
walking down a hill out by the main road. In all of the excitement, she hadn't yet noticed that he was diaper-less. "Perfect"
she thought. "Not just a runaway but a naked one at that." She
pictured tomorrow's newspaper headlines: "Footloose and fancy
free mom found dancing bra less in her kitchen while her naked
tot played in traffic".

Humiliation set in as she imagined a tiny cell with only a
bed and a toilet. She admitted to me that for a moment she
fantasized about being in a jail cell. She envisioned herself
getting a full nights' sleep, actually being able to sit down while
eating *warm* meals, with hours of quiet all to herself. As she
mused about the "freedom" in prison, she sighed, "Imagine? No
diapers, no cribs, no tubbies and with only an orange jumpsuit
to wear, how much laundry could there be?"

I thought about what she was saying. "Yeah. Exactly!" I said,
"And what's the downside?" She laughed, "Well, orange really
isn't my color." After her quick little jail fantasy ended, she
explained to the police that her husband was supposed to be

watching Garret and she couldn't understand how the terrible mishap had even occurred. "Unless of course my husband was kidnapped, or god forbid, had an accident?" she said, getting a little worried. "What other excuse could he have *possibly* had for letting their two year old run loose?" She didn't bother mentioning that Garrett was naked or that he was going through a phase where he took his diaper off any chance he got. At that point she thought, "Why even bother explaining? Don't all kids at his age strip down and run around naked?" She had heard many moms complain about this very "endearing" toddler trait.

In the midst of the near arrest of his wife, Jack strolled into the kitchen. Confused, he stood there glancing back and forth between the cops and his wife. "What is going on here?" he asked. Half smirking, the officers explained that they were in the middle of arresting his wife for "reckless abandonment and child neglect." And oh yeah, while they were at it, they may as well book the kid for "indecent exposure" too. All three of the guys shared a good laugh at that one but Dee didn't find it so humorous. As she told me, "Can you believe that? Why even joke about arresting ME, when it was clearly my *husband's* fault!" I could picture it all perfectly. I replied by saying, "I know exactly how you feel. It's always the way! Typical guys—when all else fails blame the wife."

Although their jokes weren't funny, in hindsight, it really is a good thing that they had a sense of humor. She finally got the chance to ask her husband how it was that he lost their child and he responded with, "Well, you never told me that he was heading out the door after me." Obviously, he wasn't going to take any responsibility. It was as simple as that. She said, "I watched you walk out the door with him following behind you!

I just assumed you were taking him with you." He said, "Oh, well you know what they say about assume don't you? It makes an ass out of u and me." She groaned and said, "So there you have it. Just chalk it up to another episode of husband/wife miscommunication."

After she finished telling me the story, we engaged in some good old-fashioned husband bashing and poured ourselves another well-deserved glass of wine.

I think she handled the situation fairly well, considering all the possible terrifying scenarios. I knew she wasn't even joking when she told me that the next time she decides to dance around her kitchen, she'd definitely be wearing a bra.

More than likely, a push up bra too—in case that hot, young cop has to come back someday. I like the idea of being prepared in that way. Because after all, you just never know when you might lose something (or someone) if you're not careful.

Bitching, Moaning & Griping

WHEN MY SON, TOMMY, WAS IN HIS FIRST YEAR OF PRE-
SCHOOL, a few of his classmates had mothers who decided to
organize some playtime outside of school. It sounded perfect
to me, especially since I was getting tired of building blocks
half the day with Tommy when we were at home alone together.
At that point in the game, I was his only friend. We were buds,
my little companion and me, but the time had come for him to
get some buddies his own age. Pre-school lasted almost three
hours, which left me the rest of the day to entertain my son. As
much as I loved being Slink dog in the toy story game, I was
getting tired of it. Now, if he had let me be Buzz Lightyear or
Woody, things might have been different.

It was decided that the first official play group would take
place at the home of Tommy's friend Mark. Marks's mom,
Chrissy, seemed a little schitzo to me so I couldn't wait to see
her house. Now, please don't get me wrong, I like the trait of
schitzo in a person and after a short while, Chrissy became one
of my closest friends. Even so, I had no idea what I was in for

that day. I don't think anyone did.

There were eight kids under the age of 4, and four moms including me. It was total anarchy with nothing but little boys running and screaming through the house. Even the kids who were too little to run seemed like they were ready to take flight. The energy in that room took on a life of it's own and seemed to gather speed as it did. Whipping everything around like 60 mph winds in a hurricane. I wondered where the bathroom was, in case I had to take cover in the tub at some point. There was nothing but little boys as far as the eye could see.

Everywhere you looked there were boys—running, jumping, flying, smashing—all the while banging into the walls and each other. Every time a door slammed, I envisioned a finger being caught in it. Or chopped off and bleeding.

The house felt as if it was going to lift right out of its foundation. It seemed like it was rocking, almost violently, back and forth, and every which way. Kind of like how I feel on any given day. There was no toy left untipped, no cushion was left in place and no window treatments were still intact. This once, normal looking house, now resembled a war zone. Little green army men were flying everywhere, light sabers were in motion, and transformers were losing limbs in the heat of battle. I had never seen so many boys together in one place, and at that moment, I didn't care if I ever did again. I found myself feeling grateful that my second born wasn't one of these wild creatures. I instantly sympathized with the other three moms who were blessed with all boys.

Once the main level of the house was satisfactory destroyed, they moved on to the basement, which was where the real action began. There was a playroom down there, filled to the brim with boy toys. I was positively gob smacked at the amount of toys seeping out of the woodwork. Mark's mom, Chrissy did have a leg up on the rest of us though, because she had an older boy, as well as her two younger ones. That's triple the boy toys, triple the energy, triple the boy everything. I came to the conclusion that having three boys explained why her hair always looked like she'd just gone through a wind tunnel.

While the kids were ransacking the basement, we began our attempt at a real live grown up conversation. We stood around the kitchen island drinking coffee and getting to know each another. Despite the fact that every sentence was cut short and nobody ever finished a story, we still reveled in the heaven of grown up talk. We got used to talking fast and breaking away mid sentence to untangle a wrestling match, or to retrieve a pacifier spit out by one of the babies. Even though quite honestly, I don't think any of us could say that we ever had a full conversation by the end of the two hours, we still found ourselves wanting to set up another time to meet up. And with that, our ritual was set in motion. "How about every Wednesday?" Chrissy asked. "We could trade off hosting at each of our houses," she said. We all agreed it would be entertaining, so it was settled that we'd have our playgroup every Wednesday.

We became such close friends that we carried on the tradition even after our boys left pre-school and started kindergarten. It was reassuring for me to get to know other moms who were all going through everything I was at the time. We were all in the same boat, which was a boat that generally felt like it was sinking quickly. We were treading water together, in the choppy sea of motherhood.

Then, sadly, the day arrived when our boys all embarked

on their journey to first grade. We were all so bummed. Not because our babies were leaving us but because we were about to lose our camaraderie and weekly touchstone. We weren't sure what we were going to do about those Wednesday gatherings, but we still had to find a way to occupy our younger children. The babies of the group had become toddlers and would all be going to preschool. We decided to continue with our weekly playgroup, justifying it by saying that now, it was all about the little ones. If we had any chance at all of keeping afloat in these turbulent waters, then we had to stick together.

We craved the sympathy and support that only other mothers can provide. We lived to bitch, moan and gripe. We had no desire to actually fix the problems that we complained about, we only wanted to blow off steam and maybe throw a little pity party for ourselves in the process. We knew how useless it was to try to accomplish the same thing with our husbands, because they didn't want to listen, they only wanna fix it. After all, the quicker they fix the problem, the quicker we shut up and they can tune us out. But we are women and we want to roar! Moms, with the combined strength of other moms, can do this beautifully and with minimal effort. Best of all, we can enjoy it at the same time.

Our self-made support group continued, with my daughter being the only girl in the mix. Fortunately for her, she was oblivious to the fact that she was surrounded by boys and didn't seem to miss having other little girls around.

They all played well together, maybe because they had all known each other from the time they were very young. I might even dare to say that having a girl in the group seemed to chill the boys out a bit. Chrissy's youngest son Joey was by far the busiest of the bunch. He kept his mom in track shoes. She was constantly denouncing how unfair it was that she didn't weigh ninety pounds like Jenn. Then again, she would probably be the first to admit that she might be as skinny as Jenn, if she didn't inhale a half dozen whoopie pies every night at 2 a.m. I'd bet if she had put on a pedometer, she would have accrued enough miles to have easily run to Italy, maybe even further. Joey was so busy he could literally sprint circles around the others. Poor Chrissy! That pitiful, depleted, woman got the least amount of adult interaction during our Wednesday playgroups. She was in a perpetual state of worry over Joey. He was unsteady on his feet and she lived in fear of him falling down the stairs. Almost instinctively, the stairs were the first place he always headed.

Joey also occasionally relished in eating non-edible substances like baby lotion or sunblock. Chrissy became a full time inspector diligently checking all rooms and shelves in everyone's home for anything Joey might try to ingest. He once drank an entire bottle of his older brother's shower gel and pooped red for three days. I didn't hold it against him when he managed to get into my bathroom closet and eat my deodorant. I think that may have been when he and I first "clicked". To this day, he knows he has me wrapped around his little finger. All he has to do is mention the word cookies and I'm in the kitchen baking Snickerdoodles. I suppose after somebody eats your deodorant, it's hard not to feel a sense of attachment to that person.

Eventually the Wednesday playgroup ended but I still had Joey at my house at least once a week. Chrissy and I figured out how beneficial it was for both of us to trade off. She agreed to pick up our cherubs from pre-school on Tuesdays, keep them for the rest of the afternoon and I would do the same on Thursdays. It was a favorable arrangement and we both lived for our alone time.

This was the first time in years that we could have an entire day free for ourselves. Although we missed having our weekly meet up with our fellow moms, we loved having that one day of freedom every week. Chrissy and I were able to keep this going throughout the final year of pre-school. Sometimes, we would take the kids out to lunch together on Fridays, to provide ourselves with some adult interaction. We would find places for them to play so we could sit for a few minutes of peace.

One of our finest discoveries was finding out that Chuck E. Cheese sold wine. It was cheap and flat, though undoubtedly any desperate mother's ticket to play date paradise. Plus cheap, flat, wine is better than no wine at all. Once half day Kindergarten began, we had every intention of carrying on our perfect set up. We both agreed that it was essential for our mental health. It was earth shattering for us when we found out that Joey had morning sessions and Kara had afternoons. The crushing disappointment was almost unbearable. Their new schedules meant they wouldn't get to play together during the day anymore. The real tragedy was that we felt like our freedom was being stolen from us.

I would like to say there was a happy ending to the story, except that wasn't the case. It took less than a month for me to lose my mind. Not only did I have to report to my regular part-time job as a Case Manager for adults with disabilities, I inherited a brand new part-time job as well: I was now employed as a lifeguard on the Polly Pocket Cruise Ship.

As soon as my oldest child boarded that bus at 8 a.m., my

sweet little daughter was waiting for me, calling all the shots for our day. But instead of forcing me to be Slink dog the way her brother had, she insisted that I had to be the boy lifeguard for Polly Pockets on their cruise. Since I can't wear a bikini in real life, it would have been nice to be Polly. The only time I got a break from playing Polly Pockets was when Leo, our basset hound, would come by and drink up all the pool water on the upper deck of the cruise ship.

In my heart, I knew that I needed to bask in every moment of those days because I realized when she went off to first grade, I'd miss our "one on one" time. Knowing that Chrissy was going through the same thing with Joey, took the edge off a bit. She had her mornings free but as soon as the clock struck noon, he was home again. I guess, I really couldn't complain about playing Polly Pockets because I knew that Chrissy would've killed to play anything remotely girl related. I had to remember to count my blessings. Even so, I was lonely without my weekly bitching and moaning sessions.

I often dreamt about starting a support group for mothers of young children, however, as with most of my thoughts, the idea remained floating around in my head and never materialized. I knew that by the time I ever got around to it, if I was lucky, it would have to be a support group for mothers of teenagers. Who knows? Maybe it's still not too late to get it going. Until then, the best we can all hope for is to see each other a few times every year for dinner and drinks. Unless, of course, we strike gold, which means we have a mom's weekend away—minus the kids.

Trying to plan a mom's weekend away is about the only time we decide that it's worth engaging in a complaint session with our husbands. We know that when we do, they'll think they're geniuses and that by suggesting we get away for a mom's weekend with our girlfriends, they think they're fixing our problems.

We have mastered the art of letting our husbands believe they've come up with a brilliant solution, which is a win-win for everyone. And, what could be better than that? They feel like they helped, and we get away for an entire weekend of unabashed bitching and moaning, washed down with anything that doesn't come in a sippy cup.

Of all the things I've lost

HAVE YOU EVER SEEN ONE OF THOSE BUMPER STICKERS that say, "Of all the things I've lost, I miss my mind the most"? I'm absolutely sure I qualify to have one of those stickers for my car and anywhere else people might see it. I've felt that same way a million times. Especially troublesome are the days when I am completely overwhelmed and feel like I'm falling apart at the seams. I inadvertently start forgetting things. Like when I fill up my gas tank only to realize that my purse is at home, or I have a cart full of groceries but can't find my ATM card because it's still in the back pocket of the jeans I wore the day before.

There are definitely times when I am dropping balls left and right because there are too many to juggle. So far, though, nothing has trumped forgetting my own mother's birthday. That was the day when I realized how truly debilitating motherhood could be. I might have been able to understand that kind of oversight if my mother and I weren't close, or if she lived far away, or if the actual date of her birthday changed every year like a holiday. But that isn't the case for any of those possibilities. March 24th has always been, is now, and forever shall be my mom's birthday. We have the sweetest family tradition of calling each other at the beginning of the day on every birthday. Except, one year March 24th came and went and I never made that call.

Yes, I was busy, but that wasn't why I hadn't called my mother on her birthday. I failed to make the traditional birthday morning call for the simple reason that I was completely and totally incognizant of what day it was. I'm lucky to get my days of the weeks straight, never mind the actual calendar date.

All the days and all the dirty diapers piled up perfectly until I couldn't tell one from the other anymore. Somehow it had gotten to be the end of March, yet I was mentally still trapped somewhere around the 12th. As, I mentioned, my mother and I are very close—we even work for the same company. There she was sitting at her desk on that dreadful morning as I hurried in and quickly blathered, "Hey Mom! I can't talk now, gotta run! I'm out straight today and am just here picking up my mail. I'll see you later on, okay?" Being the practical joker that I am, I'm sure she was convinced that I was playing a huge prank on her and was only pretending to forget her birthday in order to surprise her with an extravagant gift or party. She knows how impeccable my memory has always been, not to mention that I'm the family party planner extraordinaire.

It's not in my nature to be insensitive or irresponsible but there I was, whipping right by my mother on her special day without even giving her so much as a kiss or hug. if the confusion she felt in her heart registered in her mind , it certainly didn't show on her face.. Although on that day, it's quite possible it went right over my head. I ran around like a lunatic and did everything I had to do, pausing long enough only to wave goodbye. By the time I picked up my son after work, he was climbing the walls.

The weather was warming up outside, so I decided to take him to a park so he could play outside. I knew most of the parks around my neighborhood were full of dirt and would be a wet muddy mess. I thought it would be wiser to take him to the little playground right next door to my mom's house instead, which was never as muddy. He was absolutely enamored at the prospect of going to "Gramma's house". Maybe it was my subconscious leading me there? I don't know. I wish my subconscious had kicked my brain awake when I walked right past the beautifully wrapped presents on the hutch in my mother's house, gave her a kiss and innocently asked, "Hey Mom, we came to go to the playground next door. Whatcha reading?"

As she sat all comfy in her favorite chair, she smiled and said, "Oh, just the latest Janet Evanovich novel." She casually made some more small talk, politely passing the time. She must have been quietly anticipating the rest of the family's grand entrance for the likely imagined surprise party that was due to take place at any moment. But there we stood, just me and my son, not another soul to be found. No party hats, no balloons and no gifts. Definitely no elaborately decorated homemade birthday cake. My mom deserves a lot of credit because even at that point in the day she *still* wasn't saying a word. "Mom, do you feel like taking a walk to the playground?" I asked. She hugged my little boy and held his hand all the way there. She pushed him on the swings and laughed as he went up and down the slide hundreds of times.

Finally, we wore him out and we headed back to her house. What happened next will be etched in my broken down brain for eternity. I looked at my mother and said, "So what are you and Dad having for dinner tonight?" I immediately noticed a strange, almost pained look come across her face when she replied, "Oh, he is taking me out for dinner." I suddenly became confused because it was a Wednesday night. Being the creatures of habit that they are, they would never go out to dinner on a Wednesday. It wasn't adding up, although I think my instincts were finally kicking in. I said, "Oh, how come? Why tonight? You guys never go out on a Wednesday night, do you?" She was silent for a moment and then with eyes full of empathy, she reluctantly delivered the blow, "He wants to take me out for my birthday." I don't think I could have been more shocked if she told me I had missed Christmas. The myriad of emotions that ran through me at that moment was all consuming. First it was confusion, then disbelief, then sorrow, and finally profound shame.

How could I have done such a deplorable thing? How was it possible that I could have forgotten my own mother's birthday? This may not seem like such a big deal for most people but in our family, birthdays have always meant a lot. And to me, they mean everything. It was such a frightening feeling to know that the day had almost ended without me ever realizing the colossal mistake I had made. She later admitted to me that when there was no call from me the first thing that morning she thought it was odd. By that afternoon when she saw me at the office and I still hadn't mentioned it, she was certain that I was planning a huge surprise.

When I showed up at her house later in the day, she still thought there was something special in the works. She realized that I really had no idea what day it was when I asked her what she was doing for dinner. She explained to me that, "When it finally hit me that my poor baby didn't know what day it was, I knew how devastating it would be for you and I couldn't bear to break the news. At the same time, I knew that if I kept it from you and you woke up the next day realizing what you missed, you would never recover."

As my mother had just predicted, I was devastated. I immediately began sobbing hysterically and uncontrollably. I guess you could say it was as close to a full-blown panic attack as I've ever had. Luckily, there was still enough time in the day to redeem myself. I called my husband as quickly as I could and we made plans to meet at a nearby restaurant to take my mother to dinner. I ran down the street and got a cake, a card and pulled it together in the best way that I could.

All things considered, it ended up being a wonderful celebration. Despite the happy ending, I will forever be haunted by the memory. It has been many years since I forgot my mother's birthday, but I still find myself worrying about what important event I might forget next.

One Sunday dinner at my in law's house, it occurred to me that I didn't know what the date was—again. I started to panic, worrying that it might the 23rd of February, which is my father's birthday. Fortunately for me, it was still only the 22nd. My husband laughed at me when I started panicking and demanded to know what the date was. I guess it's easy to laugh when you still have your mind intact.

I wish I was able to see the humor in the fact that ever since I've become a mother, I feel like I am losing my mind, but I can't. I always think of myself whenever I see one of those bumper stickers. And I'm also positively certain, that whoever is driving the car, must be a mom. Just like me.

Leo the Fugitive

IN MY OPINION, THERE IS NOTHING WORSE THAN WINTER IN NEW ENGLAND. I've often wondered why we stay here —torturing ourselves year after year. Even though by the calendar standard, spring should arrive around the end of March, I generally don't notice my bones warming up until at least mid May.

Ever since I've had kids, I have grown to despise winter more than ever. It's bad enough when you're trapped in the house for months at a time but being trapped in the house with small children can really make you feel like you're losing your mind.

I looked forward to the springtime every year because that was when I was *finally* able to get my kids back outside to play. Even though our first few trips to the playground were always wet and muddy, it was still so much better than being cooped up in the house with a bad case of cabin fever.

One particularly memorable spring, I was filled with hope as I looked out my daughter's bedroom window and saw a tree blossoming with beautiful pink flowers. I vividly recall our first outing to the local playground that year. I couldn't wait to yell upstairs to the kids, "Who wants to go to the playground?" My son and daughter were both so excited they couldn't get to the car fast enough as they ran around putting on their sneakers. Just as we were about to leave, I looked down and saw Leo, my basset hound, staring up at me with those sad puppy dog eyes—as only a basset hound can. Partly out of guilt and partly out of knowing that he suffers from severe separation anxiety, I reluctantly said, "Oh, okay, come on— you can come too!" So we all piled into the car and headed out to have some fun at the park.

The kids played on the swings, slid down the slides and ran amuck like a pair of caged animals happily set free. I cringed a little when I saw their sneakers getting caked with mud but I knew in the end that sneaker scrubbing was a fair trade off for their being exhausted and ready to sleep. It's a well-known fact that nothing can tire out your children more than a day spent outside playing in the fresh air and every mother knows it.

Out in the spring thaw, Leo was doing his usual hound dog thing by sniffing everything he could get his long snout near. I thought he might actually wag his tail off as he relished the new scents of spring. I'm sure he detected all kinds of good doggie scents preserved underneath the melting snow. It was basset hound paradise and seemed to be turning out as a perfect day for all of us.

I'm absolutely certain I jinxed myself when I thought, "It just doesn't get any better than this." Almost as soon as I allowed myself to experience such pleasant thoughts and because deep down I really *did* believe that it couldn't get any better, things naturally took a turn for the worse.

We were only half of a mile into our journey home when my

son suddenly started to yell that he had to go to the bathroom. In frustration I said, "Oh, can't you just hold it for a little while? We're almost home."

He urgently responded with, "No mommy! Mommy, I can't hold it, really I can't! You have to pull over! Pull over NOW!" I pulled the car over as fast as I could and *of course* there were no bathrooms in sight. I suppose everything seems a little more desperate when you have a six year old screaming at you that he "can't hold it another minute." Initially I just assumed it was a routine #1 dilemma, so imagine my distress when I found out it was actually the dreaded villain #2. Much to my horror, my poor kid started squatting outside the car and he was absolutely distraught that he had to bare his naked butt out in public.

There wasn't much I could do except try my best to shield him from view. The more he yelled, the more I lost control of what I was doing and I couldn't seem to think fast enough. Did I have a towel to hide him? Did I even have any napkins or tissues or anything at all to wipe him with? I had no idea what I was going to do and he was still yelling desperately the entire time, "Cover me! Cover me up! Hide me! People are going to drive by and see me!" In my panic, I decided to open another car door to shield those little white cheeks of his.

Of course with everything going on in that moment, I wasn't thinking about the fact that Leo was in the backseat. Leo is known in our family as "The Fugitive", because he will run away any chance he gets. He certainly isn't the smartest dog we've ever had but we love him just the same. My hands were tied while I stood there totally helpless watching my precious Leo bolt out of the car and literally head for the hills. We were so far away from home I was sure he was a goner.

Basset Hounds are notorious for picking up a scent and following it for miles, so off he went. He ran as fast as those four little legs could carry him, with his big long ears flapping in the wind. He was thrilled to be free. Who would have thought those short little legs were capable of such a high rate of speed? I managed to get my son back into the car and cleaned up in record time so that we could go off in hot pursuit of Leo, with my stomach in knots the entire time.

All I can say is that luck was definitely on my side that day because we drove up around the corner and we spotted Leo with his nose to the ground. I pulled the car over, quietly tiptoed up behind him, dove to the ground and grabbed ahold of his collar so tight that I nearly strangled him.

As the poor dog gasped for air, I loosened my grip and lifted his long, muddy torso into the car. I was so grateful to get him back that I didn't even bother yelling at him. I'd thought for sure we'd never see his sad basset eyes again. I thanked my lucky stars that he was back in the car and we headed home both tired and relieved. What a day at the park that turned out to be!

I learned three very important lessons that day. First: *do not* attempt to take the kids AND Leo to the playground together. Second: *always* carry toilet paper or wipes with you even if your kids are past the age of potty training. Third: *never* underestimate the power of short, little legs or the overwhelming desire to run free.

The Elephant in my Purse

IT'S EXTREMELY INCONVENIENT for me that my children seem to be equipped with some kind of built in sensors, which always alert them to the fact that I'm in a hurry. It never fails that the few times I have plans to socialize and am actually trying to get somewhere on time, my kids always find a way to keep things moving at the pace of frozen molasses.

Take, for instance, the time I was an hour late to meet some of my single girlfriends for lunch. That morning, I half expected my then 3-year-old son to look at his over-sized Mickey Mouse watch and say, "Oh what a shame mommy! Did you know you're now thirty minutes late for your lunch with the girls and oops, I just accidentally kicked over the dog's water bowl?" He was already a superb inventor at the young age of three.

Back then I was certain he had a blueprint hidden somewhere in the house outlining all of the particular potential plans and schemes he might decide to implement to fumble up my day.

The kid never seemed to sleep, so I figured he must work into the wee hours of the night on his fiendish plots. I can see him looking over his notes, laughing sinisterly, "Just wait till she sees what I've got in store for her today...Mwahahahahahaha!!" I used to be so naive to his tricks and never imagined he did anything *on purpose*. I actually believed that it was an accident when he kicked over the dog's water bowl. It was only after watching him strategically walk forward with his foot aimed directly at it, that I realized what a master mind he truly was. He would giggle wildly when he saw the water swish-swash from side to side, splashing all over the floors and cabinets. He then delighted in watching a gigantic puddle form into his own little mini tide pool right there on the kitchen floor.

My son has always been very detail oriented and when engaged in spilling the dog's water bowl, he always made sure to have on socks when he performed this delightful and adorable act. He would sop joyfully through the puddle—squish squash—while making a trail of wet footprints right to his bedroom. At least that particular antic saved me an extra trip since the "time-out chair" was placed in that same general vicinity.

I'm still trying to figure out why he never dumped the dog's food bowl out all over the floor. Since nothing ever eluded him, I'm sure he had that idea somewhere on the blueprint, but had been saving it for when he really needed to up the ante. Luckily, he eventually outgrew that particularly winsome stage and it's likely that although he still has those blueprints stashed somewhere, he has long forgotten about them. At least I hope that's the case.

Back in his busy toddler day, while he was actively slopping around with his socks in the dog water, it appeared that his baby sister was plotting and scheming on her own as well in order to contribute her own brand of mischief to make me late.

Of course, it could also have been that she resented the fact that I was shoveling globs of pasty orange baby food into her tight-lipped mouth with a vengeance. "Vroom, vroom! Here comes the car, open up the garage door! Vroom, vroom, vroom..."

With each spoonful that went in, I watched while twice the goo came bubbling back out. It slowly dripped down her chin and plopped onto her "I Love My Daddy" bib. Foolishly, I would try to distract her with more silly games. She'd look up at me as if to say, "Keep dreaming lady! The garage closed long ago. Now please take your car somewhere else. Oh and by the way? The runways are shut down too, so go fly your plane into some other kid's mouth. Good day to you, Madame."

She must have figured I wasn't tuned in enough to her baby lingo back then. In order to sufficiently drive her point home, on the day I was rushing to get out of the house on time to meet my friends for lunch, she shoved two fingers into the jar of baby food and flung a giant glob of gooey, orange, gunk right into my hair. I had no time to worry about my hair, because her precious face was covered in the orange goo as well.

Initially, I'd thought about soaking a washcloth with some sweet smelling baby wash to clean my angel's face. Then I thought better of it and dropped that sticky, globby, bright, orange mess right where she belonged that morning—in her daddy's lap. After all, her bib wasn't professing any love for mommy, so I figured daddy ought to clean her up. There wasn't any time for apologies that morning. I shook my screaming son off my leg and ran out the door to meet my girlfriends for lunch.

A slight, *slight* twinge of guilt hit me as I left my house but it was instantly wiped away as I opened up the car windows to breathe in the fresh air of freedom. As the wind went whipping through the open windows it also seemed to fumigate the car of all "non-descript" fumes. The kind of smells, it seems, which are only possible for children to leave behind in a car. I suppose I was also hoping that if the wind was strong enough to freshen up the car, it might also be strong enough to blow the squash (or was it sweet potato?) right out of my hair. Whatever orange vegetable it was, it was gross and sticky. At that point, it was also matted into my hair. I drove as fast as I could and was crazed at how late I was going to be for lunch.

Even a fashionably late person such as myself was pushing my luck that day. I thought for sure my friends would be annoyed with me. I could feel the sweat beading up under my arms and on my forehead as I flew into the restaurant at light speed. Thankfully, I immediately spotted my friends sitting at a tall table in the bar area. They all looked incredibly put together, while I stood there feeling completely taken apart. But oh! How I loved seeing them, even if I did have to suffer through my momentary envy for their carefree lives. I watched my friends sipping their Watermelon Margaritas and I suddenly started to miss the life I had before motherhood.

There they were, happily gabbing away, bubbly and light-hearted. I could see that my friends were still the same silly girls they'd always been. I, on the other hand, wasn't the same at all. Except, of course, for my habitual lateness. As I approached the table that represented my old life, I instantly felt alienated from their single lives and baby-free world. I was vastly different now...so very different indeed. I imagined what must have been running through their minds as they saw me hurrying into the restaurant all disheveled and sweaty. I prayed they wouldn't notice the orange goop oozing from my hair and I wondered if they were thinking, "What the hell happened to her? Was she abducted by some type of Mommy UFO?" As this thought unraveled in my mind, I envisioned myself being dragged off into a giant spaceship while hugely pregnant aliens strapped me down on a stainless steel table to rob me of all that I once was, and everything that I had ever been. I imagined my friends saying, "Why did they take her makeup away? What happened to her tan? Why is she wearing those frumpy clothes?" Who would have thought that seeing my single friends sitting up at that table by the bar, looking so damn dazzling would send me into a full-blown Schizophrenic attack?

I knew if anyone could rescue me from my sudden distress, it would be my friend Ann. She would definitely be able to sympathize with my phobia because she suffers from mental illness herself. When it comes to battling demons, Ann is a pro. I also knew that if she happened to be short on words of wisdom, she'd surely have plenty of prescription drugs in her bag. She laughed when the first words out of my mouth were, "Hey, having that second baby made me a little post-partum-paranoid-psychotic, got anything there in your bag for that?"

Thankfully, before she had time to answer, I looked up to see the bartender glancing at me. "What can I get you to drink?" he asked. I stared at him and said, "Well, I was gonna have a Merlot. Except today is no longer a Merlot kind of a day, so I'll take a Grey Goose Martini instead. With extra olives." One sip and I knew his cocktail mixing skills were as impressive as his good looks. I couldn't tell if he was being cocky or insecure when he casually asked, "How'd I do?"

My answer was more truth than poetry when I said, "You make a killer Martini, so right about now, I'm in love with you."

I admitted further that, "The only possible way I could love you more right now would be if you told me that you're also a Doctor and that if I tip you heavily enough, you'll be happy to perform a tubal ligation on me tomorrow morning in your office for free." Being a bartender, I'd bet he's heard all sorts of outrageous lines on a daily basis. Although, judging by the look on his face, I could tell I had really shocked him. I was actually impressed that, for a guy, he got my joke as quickly as he did. I was both proud and amused with myself when he laughed as hard as he did after I said it.

As the vodka did what vodka does, I started to unwind. I listened intently as Mindy told us all about her new boyfriend who was a drummer in a band. "You guys know me," she said, "I've never been one for rocker types, but there's something about this guy—I can't get enough. There's only one problem though, he said he's never getting married." There was a disturbing emphasis on the word, NEVER.

Leave it to my friend Meg to dump a bucket of water on poor Mindy's fire as she scolded, "For God's sake Mindy! What are you wasting your time for? You're gonna be 41! You complain all time about your clock ticking, aren't you afraid that your eggs will dry up while you're waiting around for this clown to change his mind?" We all laughed. Well, all of us laughed except Mindy, who seemed to be turning the words over in her head as rapidly as she was twirling her hair. Eventually, she said, "My eggs aren't gonna dry up. He's totally into me. I know he'll change his mind someday. Maybe he *says* he's perfectly content just to bang on his drums all day but trust me, he likes banging me too." She laughed at her own joke and continued with, "He's had me upside down, up against the wall and even on the seat of his drum set." She confided this information with a "cat that ate the canary" kind of a grin. "Holy Shit!" I said, fighting off a yawn. "I can't even imagine where you found the energy to do all of that." Mindy looked at me quizzically and asked, "Huh?"

When she said that, I realized how old and married I sounded. I recovered my wits with, "Oh yeah, I get it, never mind. You probably got out of work and had a nap first, right?" She smiled deviously saying, "Nope, but I did have a nap *after* I accidentally whacked my head on the cymbals. Well, maybe it wasn't so much of a nap as it was more of a mild concussion. Either way, it was totally worth it. I slept all night and never woke up until almost noon the next day. "Are you serious? I asked, my words dripping with envy. "I haven't slept until noon since before I got married!

Even prior to having kids, my husband woke me up at the crack of dawn, just because he's one of those annoying morning people." I said in exasperation. With this, Meg broke into the conversation, "Speaking of married, you'll never guess who proposed!" Proposed? Who proposed? Where had I been? I didn't even know she had been dating anyone.

Meg is a very high-powered career woman. She's a Realtor and it's no secret that when the housing market tanks, many fine, hardworking, professionals in her field go under. But never Meg, because she has an unbelievably charismatic smile that goes hand in hand with her incredible drive to succeed. She's as gorgeous as she is resourceful and makes selling a half million dollar home seem as simple as reapplying a coat of her trademark shiny pink lipstick. Meg is all business. She keeps herself on a tight schedule because her time is her money. She's never been the type to waste either one on an unworthy man. "Well, I won't keep you in suspense," she said, "It's my business partner. He's gotta be THE most unromantic and boring guy in the world. He's obviously as dumb as he is unromantic and boring if he thinks I'd ever say yes. He's trying to sweet talk me by saying that our office rapport is so incredible, we'd be a sure fire success story as husband and wife. My God! I only slept with him a couple of times. What is he thinking?" She practically spit out her drink saying, "As if *I'd* buy that load of crap! He doesn't have a shot in hell at shackling a house arrest manacle around these ankles.

Besides, I wouldn't risk scuffing my Jimmy Choos, now would I?" At that, she stood up to show off her strappy new sandals. I couldn't even imagine having ankles that skinny, never mind wearing heels that high.

We didn't have a chance to find out whether or not the shoes were genuine Jimmy Choos before Mindy whipped her new Prada bag up onto the table. "Look at this baby." she said. "It's the real deal too, you know. No flea market fakes for me!" I mentally added up all of the money I'd spent on diapers and wipes in the past few years and realized that I could easily be toting Prada bags in every color by now.

I looked down at my own cheap purse and regretted bringing it when I remembered there was a huge green paint splash on one side. Suddenly I was embarrassed by the green paint, which formerly had been a sweet souvenir from a fun outing with my children. True, it was a darling memory from face painting at a craft fair, but not so darling while sitting awkwardly next to my friend's new Prada bag.

As my eyes scanned the table to find something other than the Prada bag to think about, I noticed Ann's fingers were working overtime while she was texting away. She was oblivious to everything around her. La La land at it's finest. More than likely, a Klonopin induced haze. She isn't the type to be concerned with shoes or handbags but whomever she was texting certainly had her full attention.

After a few minutes of watching her texting furiously, it started to annoy me. Finally I grabbed her phone and said, "Who the hell are you so into that you're ignoring all of us?" She laughed at first but admitted that she was texting a male colleague. She had unmistakable guilt smeared across her face when she clarified, "I'm so sick of beating myself up over my failed marriage. Even though I know this guy is just an ego boost, it's working for the moment, and I'm just gonna run with it." Delirium replaced her guilt when she said, "Besides, he's a bad boy and I *love* bad boys!"

After we'd heard all of the sordid details surrounding the single life, it was my turn to share. I thought to myself, "Hmmm, what kind of wild and enticing stories might *I* have to bring to the table?" What could I add to the conversation? I wondered if my single friends would want to hear about how I was spending my days wiping up urine off the bathroom floor because neither my three-year-old son nor my husband can aim to save their lives? I'm sure they would be bored to tears if I explained how I had to continually change vomit-covered sheets and do laundry all night long after my son's recent stomach bug.

Listening to Mindy's wild stories about her drummer, I thought to myself, "What had I banged recently? Let's see, I banged the lint out of the dryer filter, I banged the fridge when the icemaker jammed up and I even banged my own head against the wall in frustration wondering why my son never seems to sleep. *Ever.*

As I was contemplating what to say to my friends, my cell

phone rang. While reaching down to grab it, I spotted a big smear of something that resembled mashed potatoes on my sleeve. Before I had time to wonder how potato had ended up there, Ann gasped out loud, "What in God's name is that orange shit in your hair?" I was about to try to explain when I noticed Meg sauntering back from the bathroom looking even sexier than before. It's amazing what a fresh coat of lip-gloss can do for a woman. I immediately dug my potato-smeared sleeve, into my paint-stained purse, frantic to find my favorite lipstick. If there was anything that could provide me with a quick pick-me-up, it would be my lipstick. How was I going to find it in my big, cheap bag full of crap? Amongst the junk in my purse I had McDonald's Happy Meal toys, broken crayons, pennies, dirty tissues and a gummy worm. As deep as I was able to dig through my bag, I couldn't find my lipstick. I did, however, come across an adorable and somewhat wrinkled-up drawing of an elephant.

My son had always loved to draw animals as long as I can remember, and his artwork has never failed to bring a smile to my face. Almost at the same time I noticed my Martini glass was empty, a great epiphany struck me. Well it could have been an epiphany or might just have been a really good buzz. Either way, at that moment I realized that what Meg's hot pink lipstick did for her, my son's adorable little elephant drawing did for me. It's funny how your kid's artwork can unexpectedly and instantly grabs your heartstrings like that. I was able to look at that picture and feel totally and completely fulfilled.

Seeing my son's drawing, I knew without a doubt that I was meant to be a mom and had become truly content in my new role. I no longer needed my lipstick or expensive shoes or designer handbags. I held in my hands the only pick-me-up and valued treasure I really needed. I had almost driven myself to a nervous breakdown earlier, and for what? I had been rushing through my morning in order to admire my dazzling friends and bask vicariously in the excitement of their lives. Did I feel I had to impress my friends? Or think I could?

It was an almost laughable idea. Besides, even though my friends may have appeared dazzling on the outside, I knew that on the inside, they were no different than me. If I looked into their eyes, I would see their own set of personal struggles, pain and challenges. Sure, their struggles might have been very different than mine were on the surface, but they had struggles just the same. I knew right then and there that I had to stop being envious of my single friends, and start basking in the joy of the gifts I had been so abundantly blessed with in my new life. I called the bartender over and asked for a soda water and lime because I knew, that very shortly, I was going to be driving home.

While he was pouring my drink, I awkwardly alluded to my earlier comment. "You *do* know that I was only kidding before, right? I would never *really* have my tubes tied." He shook his head, "Oh please, believe me, there's no explanation necessary. I've got a kid of my own at home too. Why do you think I laughed so damn hard when you said it?"

I realized I had never needed to impress my single friends, because they cared about me despite my flaws or insecurities. It didn't matter to them if I wore Jimmy Choos or had a Prada bag or the latest style of jeans. They didn't care about how I looked or where I shopped. They loved me unconditionally, mashed potato on my sleeve, orange squash (or was it sweet potato?) in my hair and all.

Uncensored

IT WASN'T EASY HAVING A BABY AND TWO TEENAGERS IN THE HOUSE AT THE SAME TIME. When my stepchildren were young, they spent their afternoons and many weekends with us. While they kept busy working on middle school homework, their little brother Tommy was at that wondrous time in his development when he was learning to talk. I was overjoyed to hear him utter his first few words. I wasn't even that hurt when he said da da before he could say ma ma. I had done my research and I knew that for some strange reason, it's easier for babies to make the "d" sound than the "m" sound. It was all okay with me as long as he was talking.

Soon after he started saying "da da" and "ma ma", he was saying sister and brother and all kinds of fun words. I bought him an encyclopedia of animal words and was truly ecstatic when he could both recognize and say the word "Chinese Silk Moth". How could a mother not be proud when her little baby could impress people with such knowledge?

His vocabulary was expanding every day and I took great

joy from teaching him as many words as I could. We would sit together every afternoon and work on his words at the kitchen table. I was amazed at how fast he was learning all of the new words in his little animal book. He mastered the words from antelope to zebra and everything in between. Although I thought the "Chinese Silk Moth" was his masterpiece, it wasn't until I heard him utter the words: "Fucka Bitch" that I realized *just* how far his word repertoire had expanded.

Apparently he had been upstairs with the older two kids when a fight broke out. His eleven-year-old sister pissed off his thirteen-year-old brother and there you have it. Two glorious new words added to the mix. Naturally, as much as I tried to get him to not say those words, the more he reveled in saying them.

It became such a concern to me that I figured I should mention it to his Pediatrician the next time we were there for an appointment. The doctor wasn't surprised or even worried at all when I told him about the inappropriate word usage and he told me what I already knew, which was to ignore it. I learned this long ago in my job as a human service worker.

At work, if one of the patients had a not so nice behavior we were always instructed to ignore it and that is what we did. Somehow it is so different when it's your own kid though, isn't it? How the heck am I supposed to ignore it when my precious little boy is yelling "Fucka bitch" at the top of his little lungs? Every time he used "those" words it would send chills right up my spine. And boy, did he ever use them! Of all words I had taught my child, of all the countless hours with that damn animal dictionary, didn't it figure that all he wanted to say were those two choice words?

I have many cherished memories of him using those two

words and he certainly did not discriminate. He uttered them in the grocery store, at restaurants, and even one time on an airplane. The usage of "Fucka Bitch" on the airplane may have been the worst.

Perhaps it was because we were thousands of feet above ground or the fact that we were in such confined quarters but it was definitely one of my more embarrassing moments of parenting. I found myself trapped way up in the sky with nowhere to run and nowhere to hide.

We were on our way to Florida to visit my dad and for some unfortunate reason, which only made sense at that time; I was the one sitting with Mr. Trash Mouth. My husband was no dummy and he decided to sit with our eleven-year-old daughter. Our oldest son had not joined us on the trip because he had some important exams at school. At least that sounded like a good excuse, when the truth was that he probably knew all along what we were in for flying with this tyrant child of mine.

Not only was I a nervous wreck to be sitting with Mr. Trash Mouth, the situation was even more upsetting when I saw the man coming down the aisle to sit on the end of our seat row.

His clothes were perfect. They were so neat and there wasn't a wrinkle anywhere. He wore a navy blue suit, crisp white collared shirt, and sparkling gold cuff links. He had obviously just had his shoes polished in the airport. I'd never seen anyone so impeccable. That type of look is something I could only dream about. After all, here I was wearing jeans, a sweatshirt with milk splattered on it and my messy hair up in a ponytail. Had I even gotten to shower that morning? Based on my memories of life with young children, I somehow doubt it.

There was me, the messy haired, milk splattered, shower-less mommy, then down the aisle comes Mr. Crisp Suit and shiny shoes, with his hair slicked back just so and his tight lips formed into a straight line. Definitely no smile there but no frown either, just a straight line with no expression.

Mr. Perfect checked his ticket, and then double-checked it again, as he reluctantly sat down in the seat beside me. I looked over my shoulder at my husband and daughter and put on my best "oh god, please help me" face. But neither one of them was going to move. As it happened, they had their own problems. They were on the inside two seats in their row and in the aisle seat was a woman who could have passed for Mr. Perfect Suit and Shoeshine's wife.

Who were these people? What was it with them anyway? There she was, the female version of Mr. Perfect, with her skirt and blouse all neat and clean with her hair in a refined French twist, her makeup "just so". In my mind I was simmering with jealously and thought, "Wow. It must be nice to have all that time in the morning to concentrate on yourself." As far as I knew, she couldn't read minds, so I was safe.

My new seatmate was making himself comfy in his chair as he pulled down his tray and got his laptop situated. Once he started working, I began to worry. I had a feeling I was in for a hell ride in the sky. My son was already becoming restless and the captain hadn't even turned off the fasten seatbelt light yet. I wasn't naïve enough to expect that the plane ride would be easy and I'd prepared accordingly. I'd brought all of his baby necessities on board. I had an entire bag filled with everything you could possibly think of to entertain a fidgety kid. I had the rattles, toys, sippy cups, crayons, markers, coloring books and storybooks. You name it and I had it. I began to take things one by one from my bag of tricks, in a desperate attempt to occupy my feisty little child. We managed to get through every last trick and a full ten minutes later he was bored and raring to go.

He was looking for trouble and with that smart little eighteen-month-old brain of his, he knew exactly where to find it. Kids, even at a very young age, have this instinctive knowledge of when they are irritating somebody. He was undeniably irritating Mr. Perfect, who struggled in vain to convince himself that this wasn't really happening. He ignored us and pretended that he couldn't hear my son saying "No mama, no mama, I don't want that, I don't want this! No! No! No!" Although the plane was flying steadily above the clouds, my internal plane was experiencing so much turbulence, it was about to come crashing down any minute. I was twitching with anticipation and felt the need to get up and run. Despite my paralyzing fear of heights, I swear if somebody had offered me a parachute at that moment, I think I would have jumped.

As I tried to figure out how to get out of this situation, the stewardess came to the rescue with her big silver beverage cart. I was never so happy to see anyone in my life. I thought to myself, "I sure could use something to take the edge off right about now." I guess Mr. Perfect shared my sentiments because he ordered a Martini straight up. He actually must have doubled that order because the pretty blond stewardess handed him two nips of vodka. Either that or she felt sympathy for the poor bastard. Much to my disappointment, both nips were for him but none were for me. I would have to take the liberty of ordering my own. Under the circumstances, wine wouldn't cut it, so I went straight for the hard stuff instead. I don't know who was more relieved to get the vodka, Mr. Perfect or me. Regardless, we both had a little grin going on. Unfortunately, that didn't last long. That poor man no sooner got that beverage poured over his ice when my son decided that he was all done with the plane ride.

In one bold move, he jumped up and did a world class karate kick with his left foot. All I remember was seeing my son's little white Nike sneaker in slow motion going up in the air fast and hard only to come down at an angle knocking Mr. Perfect's martini right out of his hand.

Ice cubes were flying everywhere and the vodka went up into the air and came down all over that immaculately pressed blue suit. To say that he was irate would be a gross understatement. I am sure that a few choice words were coming into his mind at that very moment but he did not have to worry about uttering them in fit of anger because my son took care of that for him as he yelled out "Fucka bitch!" Of course, because nothing in my life is ever easy, two seconds earlier, I had just popped a peanut butter cracker in my mouth, which made it virtually impossible for me to apologize. I tried to talk but the words just mumbled together stuck between the peanut butter and the cracker. I honestly would have been better off if I'd just choked to death right there on the spot.

Now you might be thinking this was about the time in the story where my husband steps in to rescue his damsel in distress. Well, you would be wrong. There was not a chance, not even the remotest possibility, of that happening. Instead my knight in shining armor just looked the other way and pretended he had NO idea who the crazy lady and trash mouthed baby were.

I think if we had been on a bus instead of a plane, we would have been escorted off. In the end, I got so annoyed that I finally stood up and practically threw my son over the seat at his father.

Our poor daughter was sitting beside him dying of embarrassment. She knew deep down where my son had learned those words. I know she felt badly about the situation but what in the world could she do about it now? What was done was done and now we were all paying the price for it, thank you very much.

I knew two things for certain about the return trip. One, I most assuredly would *not* be bringing a souvenir home for his big brother, the teacher. Two, I knew I would absolutely be taking some of those Smirnoff minis home as souvenirs—for me.

Ponytail Fetish

I HAVE A FRIEND, SUE, WHO ONCE RIPPED THE BACK DOOR OF HER VOLVO RIGHT OFF. Her kids had missed their bus and she was frantic trying to get them all to school on time. As she backed out of her garage, she was going through her mental checklist: Backpacks? Check! Lunches packed? Check! Water bottles? Check! Seat belts? Check! Car doors shut? Car doors shut? "Oh shit!" she yelled just a little bit too late. You would think that at least one of her kids might have warned her that one of the rear doors was still wide open as she shoved the car into reverse.

The trouble with kids is that if it doesn't directly pertain to them, it doesn't faze them. And besides, they were too busy brawling in the car to notice anything anyway. When the door smashed into the side of the wall it was torn right from the hinges and shook everything with such force that Sue thought for sure the ceiling was crashing down on her head. "This is just great." she thought to herself. "School will be letting out by the time I get them there and how the hell am I going to explain this one to my husband?" Her nosey neighbor, "Creepy Al", came running out to see what all the commotion was about and offered to drive her kids to school. Luckily for Sue, he was actually wearing clothes that morning.

The last time she had run into him in her driveway, he was in his boxer briefs...and nothing else. He never offered an explanation, he just laughed sardonically and with a lispy, lilting accent said, "Oh my! Looks like you caught me in my underwear." Here he was again, the creep she avoided at all costs, standing in her driveway offering to drive her kids to school. Surely, this interaction was the icing on her morning muffin. After Sue searched up her sleeve for a better plan and came up empty handed, she reluctantly accepted his offer.

Later that day, when her husband came home from work and noticed the missing door, he ranted all kinds of wild obscenities as he ever so sweetly called her an idiot. She told me that he had claimed, in an extremely cocky tone, that *he* would have never done such a stupid thing, not ever in his life.

Apparently, according to Sue's husband, ripping the car door off it's hinges is only something an irresponsible woman could be capable of doing. Cold and closed off to what he felt were her ridiculous excuses, he didn't care how many things she had on her mind that morning.

In her defense, I wonder what he was thinking about when he left for work that day. Most likely something distracting and stressful like trying to decide which radio station to listen to or whether or not to get his coffee at the drive-up or go inside. There's no doubt about it, husbands can be really insensitive jerks sometimes.

One day my *own* husband backed our Envoy right into our

Camry. Not once, mind you, but twice. In an astoundingly twisted sense of logic, he blamed me. I was babysitting my nieces who are Irish twins and nearly the same age as my daughter. All three girls begged me to put their hair in ponytails. They looked so darn cute that when they all chimed in together, "Auntie, Auntie, put your hair in ponytails too! Please?" I couldn't resist their request. I hadn't worn ponytails in my hair since I was about eight years old but I figured, "Why the heck not?" I did my hair too and then we all headed out to Nana's house for Sunday dinner.

My husband put the keys in the ignition and started the car, but he never took his eyes off me. I had no idea why. How could I possibly know at that moment that as it turns out, my husband has a ponytail fetish? It was really flattering. Truly. Well it was—until he backed up our Envoy and smashed right into our Camry that was parked behind us. I couldn't believe he did such a stupid thing, yet he didn't hesitate to blame my ponytails and me. If that wasn't bad enough, later that day he did the exact same thing. Again!

After his reckless driving, which of course was entirely my fault, the car acquired a dent on both sides in the back, one on the right, one on the left and it took him over a year to fix it. I should have been smart enough to take the damn ponytails out after the first crash. One thing I know for certain is that I will never wear my hair like that again!

A girlfriend of mine once showed up at my door wearing ponytails when she dropped her son off for a sleepover. I shuddered to think about what might have happened if she had actually gone into the house and talked to my husband. I felt compelled to warn her about my husband and his penchant for ponytails. She gave me a quizzical look until I explained what had happened to my poor car, not once but twice, on the one and only day I dared to wear ponies!

On the bright side, I can always make Sue feel better about her crash when I bring up my car disaster brought on by nothing more than...ponytails.

Runaway Rolos

SURELY ONE OF THE GREATEST JOYS IN MOTHERHOOD IS POTTY TRAINING. I remember when my daughter was learning to use the potty like a "big girl". She was so proud when she got her Dora underwear and the last thing in the world she wanted to do would be to mess them up. As matter of fact, she would go to great lengths to keep them clean. Even if it meant pulling them down to pee or poop wherever she might have been at any given moment.

I remember one day when she was a little too late to the potty and she left a small trail of what resembled Rolos on the bathroom floor. I picked her up as fast as I could and plopped her onto the little white seat as I reached into the closet for the bleach and paper towels. No sooner had I turned around to clean up the mess when, much to my surprise, I saw our Basset Hound Leo with his snout to the ground gobbling up the "Rolos". To put it mildly, I was horrified. And yes, I must have been a bit naive to think that my precious pooch wasn't capable of such a disgusting act. I was stuck visualizing myself showering that dog with kisses, and then thinking about where his mouth had really been.

While I stood there, my daughter started to scream. She wasn't screaming so much as she was shrieking at the top of her lungs. I couldn't even begin to imagine what was wrong with her and it took me a minute to decipher her hysterical babble. When I was finally able to make out the words, I determined that what she had been screaming was, "That was mine, that was mine! Mommy, he ate my poop!" Was I really hearing her correctly? She was actually upset because he ate "her" poop? I mean, c'mon, we're not exactly talking about her birthday cake or Halloween candy here. I didn't get it.

Once I had children, I learned early on that in motherhood, there are just some things you can't analyze. I suppose it was a fairly simple enough concept though. The poop was hers, Leo ate it and she was furious. She didn't let it go lightly either. She stayed mad at him for a long time after that. He had eaten plenty of her Polly Pocket dolls and even a handful of her Littlest Petshop pets and I guess eating her poop was the last straw for her. Believe me, I get it that kids hate sharing, but what could she really do with "her" poop other than to flush it down the toilet?

About a year after the "Rolos" episode, one of our beta fish named Zoe died. Sadly, one morning I found Zoe floating lifelessly at the top of her bowl. If only I had been more on the ball, I would've known better than to tell the kids about Zoe's fate.

A smarter mom would have hurried to Petco, bought another beta fish and thrown it into the bowl. Not this mom though! Nope. I had to tell *all*. The truth, the whole truth and nothing but the truth! Somehow, I felt compelled to make the speech, give the eulogy and finish it all off with a solemn flush down the toilet.

My baby girl took Zoe's death the hardest. She was grief stricken and bawled her eyes out for hours upon hours. I thought it would never end and I felt like a wretched mommy for having told her.

The next morning following Zoe's "funeral", after breakfast to be precise, my daughter went into the bathroom and shut the door. In the next instant I heard her wailing so loudly, she was probably heard in the next town. She was hollering and crying, "Zoe, Zoe, Zoe, Noooooo, Zoe!" I thought for sure the dead fish must have washed up in the toilet bowl and was floating there, terrifying my daughter. I prepared myself for the worst and walked into the bathroom.

Much to my relief, there was no dead Zoe in the bowl but my little girl was still screaming and crying. I asked her what was wrong and she said, "Mommy, I have to go poop really bad and I can never go again because Zoe is down there and I just can't do that to her!" It was yet another example of the things kids think of that would just never cross our minds. It's a good thing we have another bathroom upstairs because otherwise my daughter could have developed some serious bowel issues.

Fortunately for me, "Rolos" aside, my daughter was fairly easy to potty train. My son, on the other hand, was anything but easy. For some reason he found it necessary to strip down completely naked every single time he had to use the bathroom. This lovely habit was not only reserved for home but utilized out in public as well. I remember one particular incident at the public library, when going to the potty was an ordeal.

We were at the library for movie night, which was sponsored

by my son's school. And just because he's *my* kid, he had to go to the bathroom right in the middle of the movie. Into the bathroom we go and off come all of his clothes, piece by piece. The worst part was that he refused to let me in the stall with him, so all I could do was stand there, watching in dismay, as my son's nice clean clothes are now lying all over the filthy germ infested bathroom floor of the public library. I hated thinking about having to put those clothes back on him after they'd been on the bathroom floor, but what else could I do? The days of bringing extra kid's clothes wherever I went were long gone. I hadn't anticipated that he would have to strip down like that right there in a public bathroom. I really did think he'd reserve that habit for home.

Public toileting accidents can be some of a parent's worst moments. I know that one of my friends told me that her son had an accident as she was walking him into preschool. She felt grateful to be with him when it happened and she figured she could at least save him the embarrassment of his teacher's finding out about it.

There she was, in the preschool bathroom crouching down into those itty, bitty stalls, while doing her very best to slide the dirty Scooby Doo undies off without smearing poop all over his legs. She cleaned him up as fast as she could and threw on his spare pair of undies. When she had finished cleaning up the evidence, she then needed to figure out how to smuggle out the dirty underwear without anyone noticing.

Throwing them in the trash was out of the question because her son was having a fit telling her she had to take them home and wash them. "They're my favorite, mom! Please, please, please just take them home! You have to take them home and wash them! They're my favorite, mom, please!" His cries were growing louder and louder. She had to get out of there quickly because the kids were starting to filter into their classrooms. Her little boy was frantic and was insisting that she hide the dirty pair under her shirt. And *of course,* of all the things to be wearing for such a mission, she had on a thin short-sleeved t-shirt. It just figures that was the day it had to be steaming hot outside. She could only imagine how much easier the job would have been with a nice big coat to hide them under. It simply wasn't in the cards that day.

Desperately, she stuck the dirty Scooby Doos into a plastic bag and adhering to her son's desperate pleas, she crammed them under her shirt. Oh the lengths we will go to protect our little darlings! She then had to do the walk of shame passing all of the teachers in the hallway with this big, smelly, bulge sticking out of the side of her t-shirt.

She could smell the trail of stink she was casting behind her as she walked toward the door. She said she knew they were looking at her like she had ten heads but she didn't care because her son was standing there with them and there was no way in hell she was going to humiliate him.

So, while his teachers' waved goodbye, she smiled and waved with one hand while the other remained firmly holding the bag of dirty undies secure in its place! She laughed to herself as she thought the only thing that could have been worse that morning was if *she* had been the one who had the accident!

The Spilling Gene

WHEN I WAS A LITTLE GIRL, MY MOTHER ALWAYS USED TO TELL ME NOT TO CRY OVER SPILLED MILK. Little did I know how much *actual* spilled milk I would come into contact with when I myself became a mother.

Seriously, if I had a dime for every spill I've wiped up over my long career in motherhood, I could quit my other job as a social worker and get by just fine. Not a day passes when I'm not absorbing something, somewhere. If it's not spilled milk, then it's spilled food, toys, bikes, tears, bodily fluids, and even the occasional fishbowl. Give me bodily fluids any day over a fishbowl spill. There's nothing like trying to grab a squirming, slimy, fish off the floor and then attempting to throw it back into the bowl before it dies. Yuck!

I've heard an expression that "a mom is a human napkin", which sums it up pretty eloquently. I am constantly getting something squirted, squished, wiped or smeared on me. If it's not the kids wiping their faces or their hands all over me, then it's the dirty basset hound shaking his head from side to side sending a giant string of drool right onto my pants. There's no doubt about it, raising children is probably close to being 85% maid service. Motherhood is a dirty job, but *somebody* has to do it!

I was invited to a wedding when my first child was only six months old and I can vividly recall being completely irritated when I realized I had a giant, orange squash smear on my dress. That situation was the epitome of mom as a human napkin. I do feel that the more time goes by, the more seasoned I get with my quick clean up abilities. I usually have a towel ready even before the cup falls over.

When my daughter was four years old, she actually spilled stuff so often that we affectionately called her "Spillarella." When she was still in her "Spillarella" phase, we took her to a party with a bunch of adults who had not yet been blessed with the great pleasure of having children.

The hostess thought she was so adorable and couldn't wait to give her a big, gigantic cup full of red juice. She set up a small TV tray for her and put the big cup of red juice right on top. This was a kind gesture and I'm sure it would have been fine if the tray had been in the kitchen with the nice spill-friendly tile floor, but that wasn't the case. Instead, the tray was set up in the living room and placed right over a beautiful (and spotless) *white* carpet.

My husband and I just looked at each other like, "Okay, who's gonna get that cup and how fast?" Having the mom reflex, I got up, grabbed the cup, took it in my hand and held it nice and safe—away from Spillarella and that white carpet. All the "kid less" people in the room looked at me like I had just graduated from "Mean Mom School". Their judgmental stares made me feel like the biggest witch going, so I thought I should explain that the cup wasn't safe and that it was an invitation to be knocked over. They still didn't get it. They were saying things like, "Oh, we don't mind, really! It's only a rug! Relax! If it spills, it spills." It was becoming very obvious to me that they didn't understand my daughter's glorious spilling abilities.

I was at a loss for words and I knew that it was only a matter of time before she was gonna send that damn cup sailing through the air while I watched helplessly as bright red juice splattered everywhere. I didn't want to give the cup back and I didn't know what else to say without making myself look like even a bigger witch.

My husband must have seen my frustration, because he was the one who spoke up. He isn't afraid to tell people like it is and he somehow always finds a way to make it into a joke. For some reason, nobody seems to care how direct and unfiltered he can be. By the end of his comments, even if I'm completely embarrassed, people are laughing. He looked at me and said, "Don't even *think* about listening to these people! Keep that cup right where it is, safely in your hand because we don't call her Spillarella for nothing." Everybody in the room laughed and my daughter was quite content to play with their little dog and let me hang onto her big cup full of red juice.

I held the cup for the rest of the night and we made it through without her spilling so much as a drop. Again, my husband started in with his "tell it like it is" comments. "See? Now we are leaving and you still have a beautiful white carpet. If you'd had it your way, she would have painted it red with that juice." Everyone was amused—except me. I wanted to get out of there while the getting was still good. I figured it was only a matter of time before Spillarella found something to knock over. She may not have actually spilled anything but I was sure she was gonna kick the dog, crumble a cracker on the rug or do *something* that would make our hosts think twice before having us back. It was just to good to be true that nothing was awry before we left.

Every parent knows something is bound to go wrong after a few hours of perfect behavior. I gave my husband the look to say, "It's time to go! Let's get out of here unscathed!" I got up quickly and when I did, I lost my balance and almost knocked over my chair. In a desperate effort to save myself from falling, I grabbed the side of the entertainment center and what happened next is just too humiliating not to be true.

I watched, in what seemed like slow motion, as my daughter's cup, which was still in my hand, went sailing in the air. It felt like all time stood still as it came back down splattering red juice all over the television and walls with it ultimately coming to rest on the nice white carpet.

The spilled red juice looked like blood. With the splattering of red all over the walls and a giant pool of it all over the carpet, the room resembled a crime scene. All we needed was a little yellow caution tape and it would have been the ideal set for a CSI episode.

What could I say? This was classic. The room was dead silent. Nobody uttered a word but I could read their minds as they thought, "Oh look at that, the mean untrusting mom who wouldn't even let her little girl hold the juice, just spilled that very juice all over the place!"

At that moment I was so humiliated, I wanted to die. Finally my husband broke out with, "Well, now we all know where Spillarella gets it from, don't we?"

As I found myself mopping up yet another spill, on the verge of tears, I was struck by the irony of it all—if only it had been milk. At least then it would have matched the carpet!

Fancy Pants

It was early on a Wednesday morning and already my day had been nothing short of insane. My younger child flipped her cereal off the counter. I watched in dismay as the bowl crashed to the floor, splattering milk all over the bar stool on it's way down. All I could do was blankly stare as the soggy, wet cheerios found a new home on what became a soaking wet seat cushion. In any other house, there would have been a hungry dog eagerly waiting at the bottom of the chair to lap up the mess—but not at my house. It just so happens that Leo hates cheerios and milk. Two dishtowels and fifteen paper towels later, I was finally finished sopping up the Cheerio disaster.

Meanwhile, my then first grader was upstairs screaming at the top of his lungs, "Mommmmm!!" Why was it that he always felt the need to scream as though I'm totally and completely deaf? How is it that he hadn't figured out that I wasn't answering him for a reason? It doesn't matter what lessons I actually *thought* I was teaching him when I ignored his bellows, he continued to wail until I would reluctantly climb the stairs only to find out what my next mess to clean up was going to be. With every step I took, I continued to hear the word "Mom" over and over.

That morning, by the time I reached the top of the stairs, I had counted nine "Moms." My ears were ringing and my head was pounding from the din of "Mom!" when I finally walked into his bedroom. I found him sitting on the floor wearing nothing but his underwear. I could tell by the scowl on his face that we weren't going to have a pleasant conversation.

I tried to remain calm as I asked him what the problem was. He said he couldn't find any pants that he liked. I thought, "Hey, no problem! Mom to the rescue!" I dared to think that it would be a quick fix and that I'd solve the problem in record time.

I smiled proudly as I told him, "As luck would have it, I actually just bought you some beautiful khakis at Old Navy yesterday and they are going to look *so* great on you!" I triumphantly pulled the new khakis out of his drawer and he immediately started shaking his head back and forth saying, "Nope. No way! I am not wearing those! Not a chance! No!"

I was obviously confused and asked him, "Why? These are nice pants and I spent a lot of money on them! Now stop yelling and put them on." He scrunched up his nose and bottom lip in utter disgust, as he pulled on the clearly offending pants. He seemed to be in agony once the pants were on and one second later, he ripped them off saying, "Mom, I can't wear these pants to school! These are fancy pants."

I was now completely baffled and said, "What are you talking about? What the heck are fancy pants?" He looked at me like I was the dumbest mom on the planet, "Trust me Mom, they are and I can't wear them! They have an orange line on the inside of them and they're fancy." I had to check this out for myself and I could see what looked like an orange line of trim running down the inside of the pant legs.

Now I was ready to tear my hair out—or shake him—as I began yet another attempt to fix something that somehow I knew couldn't be fixed. Don't ask me why this child of mine had such a blatant opposition to an orange line inside his pants. And who the hell was going to see that line anyway? I don't even know if that orange line was what qualified the pants to be "fancy pants" or not but I did what I imagined any desperate mother would do under the circumstances: I grabbed a pair of scissors and started cutting at lightening speed. I felt as though all common sense had been drained from my brain while I was cutting away. The thought never even occurred to me that despite the fact that I was cutting out that orange lining with a vengeance, the pants might still be considered "fancy" when I was finished.

There was no time to analyze the situation. I completed the job at hand and the orange line was successfully removed. My son may not have been *totally* satisfied but at least he was willing to wear the pants. I suspect he thought the pants were still "fancy" but at least with the lining gone, he was happy and that's all that mattered to me.

Even now, years later, I can still clearly see those "fancy pants". I will never forget sitting on his bedroom floor cutting out the orange line in the nick of time, because that morning, my son ran out the door just as the bus pulled up. I remember breathing a huge sigh of relief as that bus door opened and scooped up my little Mr. Fancy Pants and carried him off to school.

Reflecting back on that day in a slightly less frayed state of mind, emphasis on "slightly less", I would venture to guess that the lining might have physically bothered him. I also know that prior to that day, the only time he ever wore khakis was for holidays or special occasions. Maybe when I asked him to wear them to first grade, it was too confusing for the poor kid? Or perhaps he was simply trying to drive me over the edge?

There are times when I do think that maybe kids have a secret manual hidden somewhere called something like, "101 ways to drive your mother insane". Where else could this stuff possibly come from? I mean really? Fancy Pants? Seriously? Days like that made me fear the future. I sat down that day after the bus pulled away from our house and wondered, "Do I even dare to ask what's next?" I discovered soon enough that I didn't need to ask because there were many other "pants" dilemmas in the years to follow.

There was the time he told me that he couldn't wear "soft pants" to school because "certain things" can happen to a boy that might be embarrassing. Of course, against my better judgment, I couldn't let it go at that. I probed further to find out what, in my gut, I knew I really didn't want to know. Why didn't I follow my own mother's good advice? She had often said, "Don't ask the question, if you don't want to hear the answer."

I looked at him quizzically as he explained that "his weenie sometimes gets hard when he has to pee really bad and if he has soft pants on, then the other kids will see it." I was literally speechless when he asked me if his doctor could remove "the bone." I have to say, that little bit of candor threw me for a loop. I never expected anything like that from a third grader. I decided it was just best to leave that one alone and let him steer clear of soft pants.

I'm not even sure at this point what he meant by "soft pants" but I assumed they were a variation of "fancy pants". I somewhat recall it being "Pajama Day" at school once and I couldn't understand why he didn't want to show school spirit and had refused to wear the requisite pajamas. Well, now I know. And believe me, I truly wish I didn't.

Another "pants problem" was the time when he refused to wear any light colored jeans. For the life of me I couldn't understand what that was all about. He finally admitted that he thought all of his light colored jeans made his thighs look fat. After *that* confession of his, I thought I had officially heard it all. I might have expected a comment like that from a fifth or sixth grade girl but my third grade son? That totally came out of left field. My husband tried to explain to him that actually, it's a good thing for boys to have larger thighs—*especially* if they wanted to play football. Even with that kind of reasoning, he still wasn't having any of it. Now mind you, the whole "fat thighs" idea was coming from an average sized kid who has always had an ideal weight and height for his age.

I found the whole issue around pants all a bit over the top. I resolved to help him find pants that weren't fancy, didn't have a lining, weren't soft and didn't make his thighs look big. If I am ever to find the pants that meet all criteria, I will buy a pair for every day of the week.

Hopefully finding the "right" pants will solve the problems we've had over the years due to the "wrong" pants. That solution may sound like the easy way out but it seems it would probably be the best way to relieve my stress about my son's issues around pants. Not to mention how much it would relieve *his* stress about his issues around pants.

Whatever solution we come up with, no matter how wacky an idea it might be, if it relieved my son of this unnecessary stress we'd do it in a heartbeat. Any pants we could get to do that? Well, it would definitely be worth it. *Definitely.*

Caught in the Act

ONE DAY I PULLED UP TO MY DAUGHTER'S PRESCHOOL, LATE AS ALWAYS, although still blissfully happy to be dropping her off in order to have my two hours and forty-five minutes of sanity. Okay, maybe using the word "sanity" is a stretch. I've never been sane, even BEFORE kids. But sane or not, two hours and forty five minutes of freedom was all mine! My friend/ partner in crime, Chrissy, had a child in the same school, so we often ran into each other in the carpool line either when we were dropping off or picking up. We always looked forward to checking out one another's morning "ensembles".

Her best look by far had to have been when she wore her big, striped, fuzzy, red socks with the Capri sweatpants, an over sized hot pink sweatshirt off the neck, which was just enough to cultivate that early '80's "Flashdance" look, topping it all off with her blond hair sticking straight up all over the place.

She had equal affection for my "Life is Good" pajama pants with the "steaming coffee cups" print, mismatched with one of my husband's sweatshirts. Of course the look wouldn't have been complete without the pink Red Sox cap gracefully covering up my messy, morning bedhead.

All of the drop offs at school were pretty much the same everyday. We'd pull up in the line, wait for the teachers to take our kids away and do the happy dance, while we drove off smiling from ear to ear.

For some reason, on one particular day, there was a hold up at the top of the line and I was caught at the bottom of the hill. I was trying to see what all the commotion was about but I couldn't see a damn thing. I decided to open my door and step out to get a better view. When I did, I spotted Chrissy up at the front of the line. I was overjoyed at the mere sight of her, half out of her minivan, with her son Joey trying to tear her shirt off. She struggled fiercely to free herself of the little tyrant, but unfortunately, she wasn't having any luck. She looked immensely relieved when two teachers finally came out and pried him off of her. If I didn't know better, I'd think he had stuck himself to her with gorilla glue.

"So, *this* is what the big hold up is all about." I thought to myself. Even though the incident with Chrissy and her son seemed to be over, cars still weren't moving in line. Finally, after waiting for what seemed like years, a car moved up slightly and I could see a delivery truck blocking the road. No wonder no one was getting through! What the hell was his problem?

That poor bastard was about to have an onslaught of irate mothers lunging at him any minute. If he knew what was good for him, he needed to get out of that line fast! Sadly, he had no idea he was committing a crime far worse than any known traffic violation. He was cutting into our children's preschool day, thereby violating our right to a few hours of free time. He would have been better off getting a ticket from an angry cop than falling victim to the wrath of a bunch of stewing mothers. I was beginning to steam more than the coffee cups printed on my pajama pants and if he didn't move his ass soon, I was gonna kill him myself.

As I was about to get back into my car, I thought I saw Chrissy looking down the hill at me. She was disoriented after they carried Joey off but I figured she spotted me, so I started waving. She didn't wave back though, which wasn't like her. Then it hit me that she wasn't even looking at me, not at all. Chrissy was in her own little world where she spends the majority of her time...far, far away on planet Chrissy.

When she didn't wave back, I should have known better and just stopped trying to get her attention. I really should have been smart enough to turn around, get back in my car and wait to move up the line. I have no idea why but that morning, something came over me and I couldn't control myself. I started jumping up and down while waving my arms like a maniac. I suppose I thought if I jumped high enough and waved my arms fast enough, Chrissy would snap out of her trance and see me.

Unfortunately, the only person who noticed my grand gesture of affection was a dad who happens to live on my street and was dropping his kid off behind Chrissy. At that moment, time stood still. My arms were already in motion and I couldn't stop them in enough time to avoid my neighbor seeing me. I watched a huge grin glide across his face as he waved back. He probably had no idea that Chrissy was one of my best friends and there was a good chance he didn't even know her.

But I could tell that he definitely recognized *me*, even though I was at the bottom of the hill jumping up and down like a lunatic. Or maybe he recognized me *because* I was jumping up and down like a lunatic? Even though I barely knew the guy, I'd have no problem giving him a friendly little wave or a simple nod accompanied by a "hello", certainly never anything as grandiose or borderline psychotic as this particular wave was. I may as well have flown an airplane over the school with a big red banner proudly flaunting the words, "You are the hottest dad in town!" I think my face turned about ten different shades of red as I got back into my car and slowly slumped down into the driver's seat. It was going to take me awhile to get over this. I just knew it. What could I possibly say the next time I have to walk my dog by his house?

The entire situation immediately launched me into one of my obsessive compulsive episodes and I wasted the entire two hours and forty five minutes of freedom analyzing what he must have been thinking when he saw me waving at him that morning. "Wow, I had no idea she thought I was *that* good looking. Who could blame her? I mean, c'mon! I really *do* look sexy in my wife beater T- shirt. I knew she was checking me out every time she walked that sad basset hound by my house."

I thought about trying to explain the situation to him, except that the more I drove myself insane over it, the less sense it made. How bad would it sound if I said, "Oh by the way, whatever your name is, the other day when you thought I was waving at you madly at the bottom of the hill? Well, it actually wasn't *you* I was waving to, it was my friend Chrissy." No, I couldn't say that, could I? That would be rude or make me look even more psychotic because then he would KNOW I'd been thinking about the entire incident all week. There wasn't a thing I could do except suck it up and live with it. Or was there? This situation definitely required expertise. I needed to call my advice hot line—fast. Which meant, naturally, that I had to call Chrissy.

I wanted to know whether or not she had witnessed me making a total fool out of myself that morning. As usual, the call went straight to her voice mail. I blurted out the entire story, probably talking a mile a minute while I did. I told her how completely and totally disconcerted I was and that, of course, I was wearing my pj's when it happened because what the hell else would I have been wearing at the crack of dawn? And yes, as crazy as it may seem, for me, 8 a.m. *is* the crack of dawn.

Chrissy did eventually call me back, as always. Except for this particular crisis, she offered zero support. I could tell Chrissy loved my predicament, probably because it wasn't something that had happened to *her*. She thought the funniest part was that I had to face him every day when I walked my dog.

Instead of dismissing my OCD episode, she fueled my already blazing fire when she said, "Oh, he definitely thinks you want him, there's no doubt about it." She told me that she knew him from her son's class and that he was a personal trainer. "Haven't you noticed those wife beater T Shirts he wears? He wears them on purpose—just to drive all of us moms wild. He must really think he's something." I shook my head as I listened.

"Are you kidding me?" I said to her as I debated what it would take to kill my pain. "Is it too early to have a glass of wine?" I asked in all seriousness. I confessed I was totally rattled and never wanted to be seen anywhere near his house again.

Eventually, most embarrassing situations blow over and this one was no different. Throughout the course of the school year, we gradually got to know "Mr. Hot Personal Trainer Dude" pretty well. We discovered he was a stay-at-home dad named John and he turned out to be pretty cool. Despite the fact that I got to know him a lot better than I had on that ill-fated morning, I never mustered up the guts to mention "the wave".

John invited us to a pizza party one afternoon for his oldest son. There were so many people there as well as a ton of pizza, yet for some reason, neither he nor his wife ever "officially" offered it to anyone. This was definitely a first. A pizza party where they didn't serve pizza? The kids were busy with a craft project and a variety of drinks were dispersed but had they simply blanked out on the pizza? It seemed really strange to me. They may have opened up a few boxes out of the ten but they never passed out plates or mentioned pizza was served. A few mothers did go over and grab a slice or two for their kids, despite the fact that no one was actually invited to sit down and eat anything.

When the craft project was finished, the kids were all directed down the stairs to the gym room for a physical activity. Afterwards, everyone went back upstairs for cake. Chrissy and I felt like we were in the twilight zone. We couldn't figure out what was going on with the pizza when suddenly they were lighting candles on the cake. Everybody sang "Happy Birthday", they cut the cake, handed it out to all the kids and when they finished eating, off they all went to play again.

The party was winding down, the pizza was ice cold and people were starting to leave. While most of the other kids were still playing downstairs, Chrissy and I went upstairs to bring our kids to the bathroom. We ran into John as he was cleaning up. He looked at us sadly and said, "I feel so badly that nobody ate the pizza. What am I going to do with it all?" I had to bite my tongue so as not to say, "What the heck did you expect you moron? You never *served* it." He practically begged us to take some home. I politely declined with, "No thank you, I'm all set". Not Chrissy! She has this problem where she feels compelled to solve other people's dilemmas. She goes out of her way to be nice and she has that "I can't say NO to anyone EVER disease". So here was helpless Chrissy digging herself right into a hole. The last thing she wanted was to be seen walking out of there with the leftover pizza but somehow, as only Chrissy could, she ended up with two *entire* large cheese pizzas to go.

We were still waiting for our kids to come out of the bathroom when all of the other moms started to come back upstairs with their kids. Chrissy's skin was turning slightly pale, as she said, "Oh shit, they are all gonna think I asked for this or that I helped myself to the leftovers." It was a classic Chrissy moment. With her big brown eyes full of fear, she begged, "Get me out of here quick! Before everyone sees me leaving with this pizza!" It was like she just shot off her own foot and was limping around bleeding.

I couldn't help but be slightly amused by her plight. I know, I know, I'm a terrible friend for having felt that way but I've had my share of being the victim in those types of dreadful situations myself. Watching her starting to sweat gave me a little bit of perverse pleasure. After all, it wasn't ME stressing out for a change! Plus, what else did I have to get excited over at yet another boring kids' birthday party?

Her desperation escalated as we were waiting for our kids in the bathroom, and I really thought she might cry. I decided that the very *least* I could do was knock on the door. Her own child may often blatantly ignore his mother's pleas but on occasion, another mother yelling will shake things up a bit. I stood there banging on the door practically shouting, "Come on Joey let's go! Do you need help in there?" I could hear the disgust and irritation in his voice as he yelled back at me, "I am trying! But my poop won't come out!" Chrissy brainstormed in vain. She quickly realized there wasn't a damn thing she could do to make Joey's poop come out any faster. All she could do was wait, hanging out there while standing in front of the bathroom, holding her pizzas. I wouldn't be me if I didn't add a little insult to injury by reminding her that maybe her husband did have a point when he told her to add more fruits and veggies to the kid's diet.

After my snide remark, I half expected to get a few slices of cold pizza hurled at my head. Instead, Chrissy just kept screaming "Joey...HURRY UP FOR THE LOVE OF GOD!" After what seemed like a decade, he finally came out of the bathroom and it was time for our great escape. As we were heading toward our exit or I should say, as I was running behind Chrissy and her pizzas, we were halted dead in our tracks by Delores.

If there had to be one mother we'd have prayed to avoid at all costs, it would have to be Delores. She was branded with the name of an old hag, yet she was young and sophisticated.

She wore her silky black hair in a bob, with her "Dooney & Bourke" bag neatly hanging from the crook of her arm. Her fingernails were perfectly painted and if her feet were killing her in those heels, you'd never know it. With one glance, she could convey the thought, "Step aside you unworthy piece of human trash."

As our luck would have it, while we were trying to make an inconspicuous departure our nemesis blocked the way. There, in all her glory, was the devious Delores. She glared at Chrissy, while she publicly declared, "Oh Chrissy, taking dinner home for the family? Huh. Well, I guess times are tough, aren't they?" The defeated expression that washed across my friend's face was painful for me to watch. I was proud of her when she at least made an attempt to worm her way out, by saying, "Yeah I guess so, John was really upset that all this pizza was gonna go to waste."

We left there and she bitched all the way home saying that if she'd only refused the offer of pizza like me, none of that would have happened. "Why does this shit always have to happen to me? I would have liked to rip one of those fancy shoes off her feet and poke her in the eye with it, that witch!" she said. I told her that maybe it was karma payback for getting such a kick out of *me* making a fool out of myself that day in the carpool line when John thought I was spastically waving at him.

Although I did admit to Chrissy that I'd rather have been cut down by Delores, than caught waving crazy the way I did that morning by a guy who doesn't even know enough to serve pizzas at a pizza party.

No matter how good he might look in a white tank top.

Cup of Chaos

IF THERE'S ONE THING THAT I WILL ALWAYS APPRECIATE ABOUT MY FRIEND CHRISSY, IT'S THAT SHE 'S TOTALLY NUTS. I always knew *I* was crazy but *her* crazy makes my crazy seem almost...normal. Listening to Chrissy when she talks is like riding the "Super Round Up" at Six Flags. I find myself spinning around and around, when suddenly the velocity of the ride sucks me up full force and has me stuck upside down on the wall. She tells me all the time that she is convinced that her life is being video taped for a reality show in Japan. If she's right, we've gotta figure out how to get it syndicated and aired over here. You couldn't fabricate the "Chrissy Chronicles" if you tried.

Most of the things that happen to her have never happened to anyone else. For example, who else do you know that has gotten their nipple caught in the back of a hairdryer? Chrissy, for one, *has* gotten her nipple caught in the back of a hairdryer. See what I mean? It happened one morning when she was blow-drying her hair. She was naked and bent over, with her head upside down. The suction of the hairdryer caught up under her left breast and sucked her nipple right inside.

Her daily atrocities and mishaps are like a drug to me. I need to hear them; it's my "fix". Without my daily dose of the "Chrissy Chronicles", I might not survive this harrowing and tedious game of life. Before I met Chrissy, I seriously used to think I was the *only* mother out there who occasionally fantasized about driving my car off a bridge—just to experience silence.

A few years ago, I started leaving Chrissy daily voice mails. Since neither of us have time for a full conversation and since voice mails are cheaper than therapy, it worked in lieu of real conversations for both of us. I was able to vent and she was validated. We were bonded together by our catastrophes, twisted sisters of sorts and it was nothing short of divine.

Many of my other friends were still living the swinging single life and hadn't yet delved into their own baby bliss. When somebody doesn't have kids, how could they possibly relate to what you are going through as a new mom? Our crazy stories might have been just another ordinary day in the life of being a mommy but I derived immense comfort in the chaos that Chrissy and I shared.

Sharing a cup of coffee was fabulous but a cup of chaos? That was even better! We became entrenched in a competition of torment. Whoever had the more horrific or humiliating experience to share was the person who won the prize at the end of the day.

One bright and early Monday morning, as I was waiting to drop my daughter off at preschool the carpool line looked deserted. There wasn't a soul around. It was spooky really, now that I think about it. The place was like a ghost town. About fifteen minutes passed until it dawned on me that I was there during Christmas vacation. How could I be so out of it? Where was my head? What happened to my brain cells? Did they spill out with my placenta after I gave birth or did the same thief who stole my sleep rob me of my brains too? If anyone else had known I was there, I would have looked like such an idiot. There I was, sitting all alone in the carpool line, staring out at the cold December sky.

More upsetting was the realization that I had failed to give my children's teachers any gifts or had even offered up so much as, "Happy Holidays or Happy New Year!" How could I have been so oblivious to all of the other mothers handing out presents and saying their holiday farewells? I thought, "Surely a notice must have gone out at some point right?" Well it wasn't the first time I'd done something so foolish and it certainly wouldn't be the last. It didn't take too long for the next something foolish, because on Valentine's Day that year I neglected to send in valentines with my poor, unsuspecting daughter.

During the holiday-week-carpool-catastrophe, I knew it was ideal material to leave on Chrissy's voicemail. I dialed her number and said, "Well here I am at school, waiting in the carpool line, but guess what? I'm the only one in line. Hmmm... could it be vacation? And since you're not here either, that means you obviously knew and didn't tell me! What kind of a friend are you anyway? I'm sure Chrissy got a kick out of that one because I know I did.

Sometimes a good laugh right in the middle of the daily grind is even better than a PRN Ativan. I would always look forward to my voice mails from Chrissy and many times I've strained abdominal muscles from laughing so hard. Yeah, right. Who am I kidding? I lost my abdominal muscles a long time ago!

It would be tough for me to pick my favorite Chrissy saga but one that I especially love, was when her youngest son called 911. Although the story itself is priceless, the message she left me will, without a doubt, remain etched in my memory forever. The pain and distress in her voice only made it more hilarious. It went something like this: "Okay, I give up! Just kill me now! Put me up against a wall, line up at least twenty men, give them guns and have them shoot me all at once because I want to make sure I'm really dead. I can't take it anymore!"

She went on to explain what had happened and had begun her tale by saying, "I was trying to get the boys ready for hockey—the bags, the gear, the helmets and the skates. So there I was, running ragged of course, with no husband because yup—he's away again! He's away in Virginia, so here I am alone—AGAIN. I'm crazed with the three boys, homework, dinner and I was running around like a chicken with my fucking head cut off when the doorbell rang. Then I yelled to Ryan, who was already in full hockey gear, to go open the door. As he opened the door he saw two police officers just standing there looking serious. Ryan starts screaming to me in the other room, 'Mom, you'd better get in here—the police wanna talk to you.' My heart is racing as I run to the door." The police asked, "Did someone call 911 from here?" Chrissy continued, "I instantly knew who the culprit was and funny enough, *he's* nowhere to be found! So as I frantically apologize, explaining it was my youngest that must have learned how to dial 911 in preschool and they said they wanted to speak with him. Wouldn't ya know? He was hiding of course, so now I'm searching my house like a bat out of hell for the little bastard! I couldn't find him anywhere and the cops were looking at me like I was fried. I finally found him down cellar hiding in the closet, so I dragged him up to talk to the police. He said he was sorry and they finally left but as if that wasn't bad enough, I called my stupid ass husband hoping to get some sympathy and guess what he said? "Oh, well I hope you didn't make yourself look like a stress case in front of the police."

Chrissy furthered her harrowing tale by saying, "Are you fucking kidding me? THAT'S what he says? That he hopes I didn't make myself look like a stress case? Oh my god—he just doesn't get it, does he?" She blurted out this entire saga on my cell phone voice mail, and I swear, she never took one breath in between sentences. Hearing Chrissy use the full version of the "F" word without spelling it, only made the message even more comical.

I saved that message for as long as my cell phone would allow me too and I played it for every mother I knew. I was devastated the day I lost it from my archives. If I had known about YouTube then, I would have uploaded it and I'm convinced Chrissy would be a millionaire right now. There isn't a mother or a wife out there that wouldn't practically pee their pants laughing over what she said and how she sounded in that voice mail.

Kids love to throw you curve balls and when they do, it can feel like most husbands spend far too much of their time out in left field. We can be the most competent and experienced mothers in the world but in one second flat our smart little monkeys can change up their game and leave us looking like amateurs.

Some of my other favorite "Chrissy Chronicles" include the day she drove straight into a snow bank with all three of her sons in the car. She'll never admit this but the snow bank incident happened because she was checking out a hot guy. Then there was the time she fell up the stairs at her son's school orientation. Of course she fell in front of all of the other parents who were walking behind her.

One time while she was getting out of her van, she tripped over one of her own kids and sprained her ankle. And let's not forget when she set her kitchen on fire trying to microwave popcorn! Another occasion she called to say that one of her boys had stuffed a toilet full of toilet paper, which caused the upstairs bathroom to flood. Dirty toilet water cascaded down into the kitchen cabinets drenching all of her dishes and glasses.

Chrissy walked into a Heavenly Donuts once and wondered why everyone was staring at her. She found out soon enough when she returned home and saw that her underwear had stuck to a dryer sheet on the outside of her coat.

While many of my voice mails to Chrissy may not have made me a rich woman on YouTube, they weren't too shabby. Once my basset hound, Leo, pulled me down to the ground when he bolted after a squirrel. I never let go of the leash and he dragged me on my back with my shirt hiked over my head down the entire length of a neighborhood road. The scrapes and bruises I endured weren't half as bad as the humiliation I felt when I realized that the entire escapade had been witnessed by the local High School football team.

Chrissy almost didn't believe me when I told her that I had also tripped and fell up the stairs in front of people while showing them my newly renovated back deck. I started to fear, that like a bad flu, Chrissy might have been contagious. Was it the mere fact that we were both parents of small children or did she really rub off on me? I may never truly know.

We've bailed each other out time and time again. Once one of Chrissy's sons had a strange creature growing out of his head. She grossed me out when she explained that it had tentacles coming out of it and she had to get him to the dermatologist right away. The kids even named the growth "Henry".

My medical anxiety sent me flying and I was sick with worry. I knew I needed to help her even if it was only in some small way. She had been planning a birthday party at the time, so I took it upon myself to run out and put together the goody bags while she was at the dermatologist's office. I put all of the goody bags together in a basket and delivered them to her when she returned home. Chrissy isn't generally a "hugger" but for that good deed? I got a hug. "Henry" turned out to be a bizarre wart and really no big deal. The simple task of making goody bags relieved her of an extra burden, and Chrissy always reciprocates in kind.

For example, one night I had to work late and Chrissy had my kids over for dinner. That meant that not only did she have her three boys to cook for but that my two kids were also added to the mix. Five kids and with no husband to help her out meant that dinner was a lot to ask—even for the best of friends. I told her I owed her big time. I had no way of knowing how soon I would be repaying the favor. It was maybe a day or two later when I agreed to babysit her son, Joey, for the afternoon.

Everything was going along fine at first. Joey and my daughter Kara were happily playing a game of cat/dog. They always played cat/dog the same way. He was the cat and she was the dog. Well that particular day the cat decided to poop, although not in the litter box (which was generally bad enough) but in his pants. Joey was calling to me from the upstairs bathroom but from the tone of his voice, I knew it wasn't good. Sure enough, when I got in there he was bent over, cheeks apart, pleading ever so politely for me to clean up the mess. I cleaned him up, threw away his underwear and kept it all hush-hush from the "dog". Knowing, as I did, that nothing would wreck a good game of cat/dog quite like poop in the pants. Even though the *entire* time I was washing him up, the damn nosey dog kept banging on the door while demanding to know what had happened to the cat. I aided and abetted "the cat" by telling "the dog" that the button on his pants was stuck and it would be just another minute until he could go back to playing. He quietly thanked me for the protection and I smiled when I saw the sweet mixture of gratitude and relief on his little face.

Later on I called Chrissy to tell her that I had not only just repaid her favor but that she was now the one indebted to me. If the definition of a true friendship can be measured in the amount of times one has wiped the other's kid's ass, well then by golly, we are definitely there.

Another thing that Chrissy and I have shared together is our emotionally stressed induced eating. She's told me that she's guilt ridden when her kids have begged her not to wipe out all their school snacks, while I'm not proud that my kids have to hide their Halloween and Easter candy from me.

As a result of bad habits, we've both attempted to lose weight in our post childbirth years. We've both tried every diet out there: The no carb diet, no dessert diet, no salt diet, the counting points diet and of course, even the no eating diet.

The only time either of us ever felt good about dieting was when we attended a weight watchers meeting where nobody laughed when other people confessed to sins far worse than anything either of us had ever committed. We nearly died laughing inside when one woman suggested to another, "To get your mind off food, it helps to take a bath." The second woman conceded that, while it sounded like a good idea, she had tried it and found that she actually enjoyed eating chocolate cake in the bathtub.

At that point we decided to refuse to buy bigger pants and became determined to get back to "normal"—not that we remember what that is anymore. I think we've both come to realize that after having children, *nothing* will ever be "normal" again.

I guess it must have been part of God's great designs that Chrissy and I would become such good friends, so that we could learn these life lessons together. We truly are learning more and more together all the time. It's always the absolutely important stuff too. For example, discovering the importance of sharing our daily cups of chaos and how much we really need and love each other.

There are very few things in this world people need more than the kind of friend you know you can always count on. Except maybe how great it is to eat chocolate cake while taking a bath.

Revenge of the Bon Bon Queen

I HAVE REFERRED TO MY FRIEND DAVE AS "MY GAY FRIEND DAVE" EVER SINCE WE WERE SIXTEEN YEARS OLD. It really didn't come as a shock when one afternoon on the telephone he told me he was gay. It's funny how looking back on it, I can still see the long white curly telephone cord dangling over the kitchen counter as I sat on the floor with my legs crossed.

I was pleading with him to borrow his mom's car. "Please, just beg your mom to let you use the car Friday night—we just have to go out this weekend!" He'd answered me nervously with, "Well, I'll try, but she's still pretty mad at me for coming in late last Saturday night." I exhaled with frustration. "Alright," I said, "just do the best you can."

"By the way," he casually intoned, "One more thing before we hang up." "What?" I asked. He said, "Could you ever give up liking guys?" I burst out laughing, "Are you for real? What kind of a stupid question is that? Of course not! No, never." "Well," he answered matter of factly, "neither could I." And that was it. With one punch, he broke out of the closet and there's been no holding him back ever since.

I started calling him "My gay friend Dave" years ago when I was single and dating, because it was just easier that way. It didn't go over well if I didn't specify "my gay friend", when I'd tell potential suitors I was going out for drinks with "Dave."

My life without Dave would be like my life without coffee bean lipstick—totally inconceivable. I know I can always count on the bare bones truth from Dave. For example, when I've completely blown my diet and my jeans are too tight, I might say to one of my girlfriends, "How much weight does it look like I've gained?" More than likely they'll smile sympathetically and say, "Oh you look great, you don't look like you've gained any weight." I assure you this would never happen with Dave. If you ask him the same question, He'd say "You better get your fat ass to the gym and stop eating your kids' French fries." It's refreshing to know that you can get an honest opinion when you ask for it.

Dave is a super successful businessman and has made some remarkably wise investments. He travels more times in one winter than most people travel in a decade. He's blessed with a compassionate heart and in his free time he feeds stray cats all over town. It's really astonishing how after selling their homes, some people can be cruel enough to leave their cats behind to fend for themselves. Lucky for the cats, Dave will come across these poor freezing animals and he feels compelled to feed them. He drives around the city with a trunk full of cat food and jugs of water.

Somehow I have often found myself inheriting the job of "stray cat feeder" during the winter months when Dave is flying off to Cancun or boarding a cruise ship to tour the Caribbean islands. I think to myself, "What is wrong with this picture? It's ten below zero and I'm driving around the city freezing my ass off feeding stray cats while he is basking in the sun drinking frozen margaritas. I suppose it's our compassionate hearts that has kept us friends for so long.

Despite all of the amazing and wonderful qualities Dave has, like anyone else, he also has a not so appealing side. He has an uncanny ability to come out with these killer insults that can knock the wind right out of your sails. When I think about it, I guess they're part of the very same quality that I love about Dave—his brutal honesty. Emphasis on "brutal."

There is a time and place for everything and when you don't ask, you probably don't want to know. Sometimes, I just wish he would learn to leave his rude remarks where they belong—in his own mean, little head. It doesn't matter if we're alone or in a room full of people, if he thinks something he's gonna unleash it. He's like a wild bull raring it's sharp, ugly horns and when it happens, all you can do is pray that you're not the one holding the red flag.

Our friend Ann got caught holding that red flag one unforgettable day. She had recently moved down South and we were all thrilled to see her when she finally returned home for a visit. Southern food had not been kind to her and she was undoubtedly self-conscious about the extra pounds she was carrying, mostly around her belly. Dave didn't miss a beat and came right out with, "Wow, you're huge! When's the baby due?"

On another occasion our friend Mindy was the unsuspecting victim of Dave's sharp tongue. She was having a terrible day and she was depressed about an upcoming birthday. She battled through a rough week at work and when she looked in the mirror, she saw stress lines etched all over her face. Despite her best efforts, no amount of makeup was going to substitute for sleep or make her feel better.

Unfortunately, her day got much worse when she happened to cross paths with Dave at a car dealership, where he was working at the time. She went in for an oil change but instead of the warm welcome she was expecting from her friend, what she got was: "Hey Mindy! You look like a tired, used up, old dish rag!" She flipped him off in front of all of his co-workers as she angrily peeled out of there leaving nothing behind but long, dark skid marks and a trail of thick black smoke.

I, like everybody else in Dave's life, have found myself at the mercy of his unkind remarks many times. He replied to my wedding invitation by saying, "Oh, I'm sorry, I won't be able to make it. But don't worry, I'll see you at your next wedding." It didn't take much guesswork to figure out where he thought my marriage was heading.

You might think that after all these years, I'd be better equipped at handling him but I'm not. Sometimes I feel like I might choke him on his own words. Maybe it's the hormones after having a couple of kids, maybe it's the lack of sleep or maybe it's the stress that turns my thoughts to violence. I don't know.

The when and where of Dave's cutting remarks are unpredictable. I was admittedly hurt by his comments about my wedding but the havoc he wreaked when he visited my new house for the first time was far worse.

I couldn't help but feel a little intimidated by Dave's visit, since his house is nothing short of glamorous and could be featured in a magazine. You could eat off of the hardwood floors in his home and his windows are so shiny that sunglasses are a must when you walk into his living room. His house is spotlessly clean in a way that could only be possible for a person who doesn't have kids. His house is that way twenty-four hours a day even if you show up unexpectedly. Believe me, I know. I've actually tried ambushing him just for the purpose of testing my theory.

The day finally came when he was in *my* house. I had just moved in, so he'd never visited before. I loved my new house, although moving into a new place always requires what seems like endless cleaning, which is always a grueling task no matter how you slice it. I could already feel the hairs on the back of my neck standing up as I saw Dave looking up, down and sideways all around my home. I felt like I was waiting for him to break out the white glove and start inspecting for dust.

Even though I had spent a good portion of the morning scrubbing and cleaning, not to mention running around after two kids under the age of 6, I knew that measuring up to his impeccable standards would be impossible. We got through the downstairs tour and then it was time to go up to view the bedrooms. That part didn't really faze me because I had just painted my daughter's room a beautiful lily yellow. Painting anything in the yellow spectrum is a challenge.

Most of the time, there's no happy medium with yellow—it either comes out looking like a school bus or the same color as the Gorton's Fisherman coat. I'm proud to say though that her walls really did look like lilies.

Well, I guess lilies were the last things on Dave's mind because he walked right in and pointed at the windows and slam! I knew it was coming and with his arms flailing in the air, the remark I'd been waiting for reared its' evil head. He said, "Oh my god! Would you look at those windows? They are filthy! You should be ashamed of yourself! What do you do, just sit around eating bon bons all day?" And there it was.

I was beyond bullshit at that remark. I couldn't believe it! Even coming from him! I don't know why I didn't just snap and throw him out right then and there. Let him feed his own damn stray cats, the ruthless bastard. I didn't though. I just did what I usually do in my own passive-aggressive way. I tried to justify that I had been painting in there and that I hadn't yet gotten to the windows. My husband, along with all of my co-workers, took the wrath from my morning visit with Dave for the rest of the afternoon. If I wasn't so insecure and if his opinion didn't matter so much, I probably wouldn't have spent the entire next day scrubbing those windows. But I did.

About a year after the "window incident," Dave invited me over to his house and he said I could bring the kids. At first I was starting to have anxiety over what my animals would do to his sparkling clean house but then I thought, "Ah screw it. Why not? Maybe it's my turn to get him back for the 'bon bon' comment."

I set my kids free in his palace and let them run wild. It was obvious, by the look on his face, that he was starting to come unglued. I figured any minute the pictures would start flying off the walls and smash to the ground. Even though the floors were shaking, nothing had broken...yet. In an effort to settle them down, Dave made a monumental mistake. He offered my darlings some chocolate chip cookies and chocolate milk.

I secretly took great pleasure knowing that he had no way of understanding the correlation between sugar and children or the events he had inadvertently set in motion. I just sat back to take in the show I knew would start to unfurl. I thought it was certainly going to make for some great entertainment. He naively handed them the cookies and milk and said, "Here you go guys, just take them over to the kitchen table." At that point, I felt it would be inhumane if I didn't tell him that the kids would be much better off outside on the deck. After all, I could take the whole revenge thing only so far.

We all headed outside and sat down on the stunning Pier 1 wicker patio set. In no time at all, the sugar started working it's magic. Up they went! Standing on the chairs and rocking the table, I watched as the umbrella almost pole-vaulted right out of its stand. The cookies were flying and milk was spilling until finally everything became just one big, wet, soggy mess. It looked like a chocolate massacre had gone down on the good ship lollipop. I was afraid to even look at Dave.

Eventually I did and I saw that his eyes were transfixed like a deer in the headlights. He was just standing there, in what I can only imagine to be utter disbelief, at the scene around him. Just as Dave went into the house to grab a broom and dustpan, my son decided to pee off the back porch into the yard directly onto Dave's meticulously landscaped grass.

Despite my best efforts to explain that it was just a phase my son was going through at the time, Dave was not impressed. Once my child finished "watering the lawn," I suggested that we should probably get going. Well, let me tell you, Dave couldn't help me to the door fast enough. He grabbed my purse, scooped up all the kids' toys and practically shoved us out the door. The poor guy even went so far as to personally carry my youngest to the car himself.

For some reason, which I cannot comprehend, ever since that particular visit, we have never been invited back. I'm guessing after experiencing kids high on sugar, he might have a little more sympathy for my dirty windows the next time he visits. That is, *if* he ever comes to visit again.

If he does come back, he'll come bearing gifts as a peace offering if he knows what's good for him. I think he really ought to consider bringing me those bon-bons. Don't you?

Say It Isn't So

WHEN MY SON TOMMY WAS EIGHT YEARS OLD, I TOOK HIM SHOPPING FOR SOME NEW JEANS. We had been procrastinating forever about it. He wasn't exactly thrilled about the trip and I can't imagine many boys at that age that would have been too excited about shopping with their moms for new jeans.

It would have been hypocritical though if I had criticized him for his lack of enthusiasm because I also detest shopping for clothes. Of course, if he hadn't been so psychotic at that age when it came to his clothes, I could have just grabbed a few pairs of jeans, brought them home, had him try them on, and been done with the whole ordeal. That wouldn't have done me any good anyway, because experience had taught me that if I were to buy jeans that way, my son would have told me that none of them were going to work for him and back to the store they would go. In the end, it would just become more of a headache for me, someone who hates shopping in the first place.

As far as I'm concerned, the fewer shopping trips I have to make in life, the better. That particular shopping excursion wasn't nearly as heinous as I had feared. We were actually in and out of the boys department in less than thirty minutes. He tried on four or five pairs of jeans and complained the entire time. Although, much to my relief, he managed to find three pairs of jeans, which not only fit him but also met his preposterous standards of approval.

I paid for his jeans and we started to head out the door, when I realized I needed to use the ladies' room. And I usually won't pee unless it's a dire emergency. My daily agenda is too full to stop and worry about my own bodily functions.

I've often found myself thinking about how useful a catheter and an IV drip of coffee would be. It had been a long time since I had used a ladies room while out shopping with my son. As a matter of fact, that day I couldn't remember the last time I had dragged him into a bathroom with me. I knew he would surely be disgruntled about going into the "Girl's Room" with his mom. At the mere mention of the word, "Ladies Room", he looked like he'd seen a ghost.

"Please mom, come on! Just let me wait outside the door, Please?" "Sorry honey." I said. "Even though you're eight now, it doesn't mean that somebody still can't try to steal you."

Deep down, I knew that if somebody was foolish enough to take this particular eight year old, they'd certainly be smart enough to return him–once they realized how high maintenance he was at that point in time.

He huffed and puffed and begged and pleaded but he simply wasn't going to win that one. He hung his head low and reluctantly followed me into the bathroom. Luckily for him there were no other women there and I went in and out of the stall as quickly as humanly possible. He was equipped with very specific instructions while waiting. I told him, "Just stand by the wall over there and don't look at anyone or talk to anyone and I promise I will be fast."

I remembered the days when he would be poking his head under the stalls surprising all of the squatting ladies. Thankfully those days were behind us. At eight, he would have rather died a million deaths than risked seeing some strange lady's naked butt on a toilet. I was confident that he would do as he was told and stand there minding his own business.

As promised, I was in and out in probably under thirty seconds. I quickly washed my hands and skipped the dryer as we hurried out of the store. We were not even out the door yet when he asked me, "Mom, what was that big silver box on the wall for?" Even though it's always my natural instinct to explain everything, I learned long ago never to offer an answer to a child before first allowing them to tell you what *they* think.

Thankfully that day my young motherly wisdom had already kicked in, so I looked at him quietly and turned the question back on him. "What do you think it is?" Sure enough, he had already formulated his own opinion about the silver box. He looked up at me and said, "Oh, I know it's for napkins Mom, on the outside of the box it spells 'napkins' with a slot for twenty-five cents. That's so stupid because there are tons of napkins on the counter right over there by the sink. This store is a rip off you know, because why would they make these poor ladies pay twenty-five cents for napkins when they are right there on the counter for free?"

I didn't argue with him. Instead, I was silently thanking God that I didn't have to launch into a full-blown explanation about what feminine hygiene products are and why moms need them.

Sometimes it's really hard to gauge how much your kid knows or doesn't know. I've never been naive about the fact that my son has always gotten quite the education from his older brother and neighborhood friends.

One afternoon, when my son was in elementary school, he barged into the house off the school bus and proudly announced that he knew what "Sex" was. I thought I was going to faint on the spot. Once again, I waited for his explanation before saying a word. He said, "Well, it's really, really gross mom. You probably don't even want to know about it, but it is when two people lie on the bed naked and kiss!" I made a face like I might throw up and said, "Ewww, you're right, that *is* gross." What else could I say? That just wasn't the right moment to launch into a discussion of "the birds and the bees". At least for me it wasn't.

Soon after that particular incident about sex, while we were at my mom's house for dinner, he casually said the word, "Douche Bag". My jaw practically hit the ground. I was telling my mom a story about a hostess who worked at a restaurant where my husband and I had recently had dinner. I had momentarily paused and was searching for the right word to describe her, but Tommy beat me to the punch when he came out with, "Douche Bag". The worst part wasn't the offensive word, but the look on my mother's face, as her normally adorable grandchild uttered this vulgar and disgusting word. I was speechless, not to mention incredibly taken aback by the entire situation.

My son is no dummy and could tell by our reactions that he had just said something very naughty. He ran into the guestroom, threw himself on the bed and began to cry his eyes out. Gramma, as always, came to the rescue and hurriedly consoled his weary little heart. She explained to him that she understood that he didn't know what the word meant or that it was a naughty word and she quickly let him off the hook. She also took pains to make sure he knew that he was forgiven. That it wasn't only Gramma who forgave him, he was forgiven by God as well. I, however, wasn't as quick to absolve him of his sins.

Even though I knew he was oblivious to the meaning of the word he had just blurted out, I was still upset. I told him never to use that word again and emphasized to him that if he didn't know whether or not a word was "bad" or "good" he needed to find out first before throwing it around at his grandmother's dinner table.

My son has been known to have a habit of saying certain things at the most inopportune of times. He thinks he's a comedian based on the reactions he often gets from his off the cuff remarks. What he's never realized is that as funny as *he* thinks his comments are, they generally cause his mother a lot of undue suffering and embarrassment. I will never get over a visit to the Doctor's office when Tommy decided to tell his pediatrician that, for all intents and purposes, I am unable to tend to him at night because I am a drunk. Not in those words *exactly*, but that was the gist. At least the way I heard it.

I had taken Tommy to the doctor for a follow up visit due to a persistent cough that just wouldn't quit. He'd had the cough for a while, despite our best efforts to clear it up. He had finished one dose of antibiotics several weeks earlier, but the cough still lingered. I was anxious for the appointment to end and it hadn't even begun yet. I was nervous, agitated and in somewhat of a negative mood before the doctor even entered the exam room. My frayed state of mind actually had very little to do with Tommy's cough because I had confidence enough in his pediatrician that we'd get to the bottom of it. I was irritated because by being there, I'd broken my own cardinal rule about taking Tommy to his doctor appointments.

After many trips to the Doctor's office that year, I had subsequently told my husband I was *done* taking our son to any more appointments. I felt like I just couldn't do it anymore because Tommy was always coming out with stuff at the doctor's office that made me want to crawl under a table. I had caved in though, and once again, set myself up for more suffering as I ventured to the pediatrician with my little wiseacre.

During that particularly memorable visit, it wasn't just the fact that Tommy told the doctor I was a drunk, it was everything else he had said in addition that had me trying to dive under furniture.

When the doctor walked in, Tommy had self-diagnosed his cough and explained that he was positive he had allergies because, "What kid do *you* know that has a cough for three months because of a virus?" The doctor subtly smirked as he continued on with the examination and asked my precocious son question after question. "When do you notice yourself coughing the most?" he asked Tommy. "Well, actually during third period at school." Tommy answered.

The doctor curiously responded with, "Really, and what subject is that?" Tommy—now on a roll—said, "Math. And I really don't like math that much." I just shook my head and silently prayed that we were almost done. The doctor began talking about dust allergies, wood stoves and other possible causes of a lingering cough. I was dreading what Tommy would come up with when his doctor mentioned that dust is the cause of many allergies. I was waiting for him to blow the whistle on me and say that there was a month's worth of dust piled up on his bureaus, in addition to every other surface in his room. Which also meant, of course, dust covered every surface in the rest of the house as well. There was also the possibility that he might say something like, "My mom's too busy to dust since she's always gabbing on the phone with her friends."

I started to sweat while I waited for the comment that I was sure would mortify me for the rest of the day. For a moment, he was contemplative and silent. Believe me, a quiet and thinking Tommy isn't any bargain either, because that is usually when he does his best work. I soon discovered I was right to be concerned. Just as I had feared, I was about to be slaughtered. Little did I know that about ten seconds after his contemplative silence, Tommy would take his best work to a whole new level.

The doctor looked at me and asked, "Would you say he is coughing a lot during the night?" I thought about it for a minute and when I started to say, "Well, I wouldn't really know because..." My son had a huge grin on his face as he launched his grenade and interrupted with, "Because she's too busy drinking beers all night with daddy!" Ah yes, there it was—the clincher! I'd never even gotten a chance to finish my sentence, which was going to be, "Because once my head hits the pillow, I'm dead to the world after being *this* kid's mom all day long." Why even try to defend myself after that little gem? It was no use. The damage had been done. At that point, I figured I had already lost the battle and I knew there was no winning the war. I looked at the doctor and said, "Well actually, I usually don't drink beer—I prefer a glass of Merlot."

I was sure the doctor was wondering which agency to call first, "Hmmm, should I call AA or DSS?" When the doctor finally diagnosed my son with a low-grade sinus infection, Tommy's response was, "Well, Doctor, what time is it?" as he looked out the window. "My mother parked in a thirty minute parking spot and we are about to get towed, so if you don't mind we have to wrap this up." I am sure at that moment my face was as pale as a ghost and I half expected to faint right there in front of the Doctor. You can bet I was absolutely looking forward to that glass of Merlot before I started "drinking beers with daddy all night."

My husband's favorite line is "We pay for the sins of our fathers" All I can say is, I know my dad is far from perfect but he must have a heck of a lot more sins that I could ever possibly imagine. When I checked out at the front desk of the doctor's office, I told the receptionists that there was a good chance that at that very moment, the doctor might be on the phone calling child protection services. Seeing the puzzled looks on their faces, I told them what Tommy had said in the exam room and they all laughed so hard they had tears in their eyes. Sure, easy for *them* to laugh, *they're* not the ones getting skewered by an eight-year-old.

On the ride home, I did try to explain to Tommy that what he'd said in the doctor's office wasn't really funny and if he says that stuff to the wrong people, they might take it very seriously. He told me that *he* thought it was a riot—and so did the Doctor. Well, so much for my attempt at curbing my comedian.

When we arrived back at our house after that appointment, I had no inhibitions whatsoever about pouring myself that glass of Merlot. It might have been a little bit on the "too early" side of day when I opened that bottle but I didn't care. Because, after all, I *did* have a reputation to uphold.

The Triplets

WHEN MY STEPDAUGHTER WAS EIGHTEEN YEARS OLD, she convinced me it was time to go shopping for new underwear—specifically a new bra—for me. She was sick of hearing me complain about my third boob. For some reason, all of a sudden, it seemed as though every bra I owned at that point was slacking off on the job. Things weren't staying in place like they used to and I constantly found myself adjusting left to right, top to bottom. It was all annoyingly inconvenient and a big nuisance, especially when I was out in public.

I remember thinking, "If only I were a guy. Nobody would judge me. I could stand there proudly grabbing, yanking and adjusting, right out there in the open." I got so tired of trying to nonchalantly put my left breast back into my left cup that eventually it just became easier to let it stay where it wanted to.

I've heard women say that one breast is always a little bigger than the other, which must be true because for some reason, the right one always behaved and stayed put. I've seen a lot of ladies walking around with the four-boobed syndrome, but for me it was three.

For the first five or ten minutes of the day, everything would be in it's proper place, but after a few hours of moving around, inevitably part of the left side would practically jump out of it's cup and peek out, as if to say, "Hey, look at me!" So it didn't take a lot of convincing for me to embark on the bra-shopping excursion with my stepdaughter. She swore up and down that she had suffered the same problem before she found the right place to shop. I appeased her, but didn't believe a word she said. Naturally, her body parts were all intact, as they haven't yet been butchered by pregnancy and childbirth.

She assured me that all my problems would be solved after one trip to Victoria's Secret where they would accurately measure me and fit me with the perfect bra. She said, "You can't even imagine what a difference an inch or two can make! Once you try the "Sexy" bra, I promise you will never, ever want to wear any other bra again." As skeptical as I was, I decided to take a chance and listen to what she said and I wearily headed out to Victoria's Secret to get measured.

As I was standing in the changing room, I could feel myself starting to sweat. All I could imagine was some young girl coming in and telling me to take off my top. The mental image was almost unbearable as I visualized the bra coming off and gravity taking over. With one swift downward motion, I would be forced to haul my boobs back up off the dressing room floor. Talk about perfect birth control for this young sales associate! I was sure that seeing my post-pregnancy boobs would traumatize her for the rest of her life. Just as I was about to bolt out of the store, she knocked on the door and told me to keep my bra on so she could measure me. Thank God for small miracles!

It's odd that at my age I didn't have even the vaguest idea of how boobs were measured or what my true bra size was. Then again, after I had my second child, even my shoe size had changed so it would stand to reason that my bra size would too.

In waltzed a perfectly proportioned and stunning young girl with a measuring tape. I was sure she must be featured in the Victoria's Secret catalog somewhere. Her long blond hair was neatly pulled back into a braid. Her bronzed, sparkly, skin was glowing, and her huge green eyes burned a hole right through my third boob. I was sure she must have been thinking, "Oh, what a pathetic mess this one is!"

Following her eyes, I read her mind. Her face said, "God help me if I ever have children and my perfect breasts fall apart like that." I could almost see the terror wash over her. I'd love to know how she kept a straight face while still managing to force a wide, sympathetic smile, because fear must have been seeping through her very pores. I suppose pity can generate that in a person.

I would bet at that very moment she was making a secret pact with God. Silently praying, "Please, God, just let me keep my perfect, firm, perky, 34B's forever and I will do anything to help this poor, helpless, triple-breasted mess look normal again." She measured me in two seconds and stated with the utmost confidence, "You're a 34C, and not a 36 C like you thought you were.

She disappeared quickly and returned with both arms

draped full of bras. Hot pink, lavender, black, and nude styles in one arm with lacy, shiny, silky, push-ups and wireless in the other. It was raining bras. She assured me that any one of the hundreds I chose would fit me to perfection. I was astonished to learn that I had actually been wearing the wrong bra size for years.

The whole size, measurement thing is perplexing to me but apparently, that extra two inches can be entirely problematic. I would surmise that those two inches were responsible for the birth of my third boob. It all made sense now. I was relieved, and infinitely grateful to this very young, yet super sensational bra connoisseur. I chose black, lavender, lace, and silk. Four sparkly, sexy, new bras and almost a car payment later, I left the store tingling with excitement.

To be so revved up over a shopping trip was completely uncharacteristic of me. I raced home eager to put my third boob to death. Unfortunately, there was no time to kill the third boob that night. Like every night, I had to get the kids to bed, fold laundry, load the dishwasher and try to remember to brush my teeth before collapsing into my own bed.

Despite my exhaustion, I was up before the alarm the next morning. Which again, was very uncharacteristic of me. I had become mad with passion over my new bras. Ordinarily, my biggest excitement is seeing the school bus rounding the corner, but not on that day. On that day, I would have my long awaited boob makeover.

Sure, I might have the same old boring mom clothes on the outside but underneath, would be a sexy lavender push-up bra. And best of all? I'd have *two* happy boobs instead of three slightly miserable ones. And hey, they might miss their third sister but who needs triplets when you can have a perfect set of twins? I was in love with this bra.

In love with a bra? What was happening to me? The new bra was evoking all kinds of new emotions in me. I wondered if maybe Victoria's *real* secret was that they filled their bras with Oxycontin. I envisioned tiny little chemicals floating out of the fabric traveling to my brain making me oh-so-content even to be doing the most mundane of daily chores.

The doorbell rang while I was daydreaming away about my fabulous new boobs. If doing dishes could fill me with such delight, just imagine how thrilled I was to answer the door! On any other day, I would begrudge whomever it was who had the audacity to ring my doorbell this early in the morning. But not that day! That day, I was a new woman! I was bubbling over with joy to greet whomever it was waiting at my front door. I opened the door to find the water meter guy.

Since our water meter is archaic, the guys still have to go into our cellar to read it. This was certainly his lucky day because if I had still been wearing my old ill-fitting bra, I would have thrown an attitude at him for inconveniencing me in this way. He apologized for the intrusion but seemed grateful for my good manners. I recognized him from the last time he read the meter. He knew my husband from high school and I have to say, he was unusually chatty for a man.

As he stood there telling me stories about his three-year-old son, I suddenly noticed his gaze shift and fixate on one particular spot. At first, I thought it must be my new purple and white lacy push-up bra working it's magic. As I thought to myself, "I'll bet I look ten years younger! With this amount

of lift, I might even look a little *hot*—never mind normal."
The extra boob had finally departed, and boy what a truly
"uplifting" feeling it was!

The meter reader couldn't seem to take his eyes off of my
chest, which at first was flattering, but now the extra attention was starting to make me squirm. What the hell was he
looking at? For some weird reason, it became pathetically
obvious that his gaze was lopsided, and mainly focused
toward the left side of my chest.

I instantly felt dread spreading through my veins at the
very idea that the third boob might be back. It was such an
awkward moment and I could feel my stomach tightening
into a knot. I wanted to flee as fast as I could to the closest
mirror in the house. I needed to seek confirmation for myself.
Was it possible that the third boob had actually *resurrected*
itself right there in front of the water meter guy? He lingered
there in my foyer while I self-inflicted myself with torturous
thoughts. It was as though I was standing on the highest
mountain frozen with terror.

I could hear myself repeating, "Don't look down! Whatever
you do, don't look down!" I knew if the water meter guy saw
me look down, it would be all over, because then he would
know that I knew what he knew. Under such circumstances,
even I, the mistress of quick-witted comebacks, would find
myself at a loss for words.

At long last the meter man left, and I painstakingly looked
down at my chest. And there it was, in all of its glory. The
infamous third boob had returned, but this time it wasn't just
the third boob peeking out, it was the third boob *and* the
entire nipple sticking straight up out of my beautiful, brand,

new bra. "Well, so much for Victoria's Secret," I thought. "Even Victoria can't save me from boob hell, whatever her secret might be."

Maybe I need to revolutionize the bra market and come up with a new size chart? How about creating a C plus or C minus? Because clearly, I'm not a 36C or a 34 C and it just doesn't seem fair to categorize all women into only four letters. Well, maybe it's all 24 letters of the alphabet now that there are breast implants, but you get the idea.

Eventually, I returned to Victoria's Secret and was grateful to consult with a bra connoisseur who was a little closer to my own age and had also given birth to a couple of children.

Unfairly enough, she still looked undeniably sexy and I secretly wondered if she was possibly lying about having had kids. She made some worthwhile suggestions on a bra that she claimed was guaranteed to make my boobs behave. It's called 'full coverage', yet supposedly still sexy. As if I really care about sexy?

Because believe me, I can tell you there is nothing *less* sexy than having your nipple fall out of your bra right in front of the water meter guy.

Bite Me

I **FIND THE GENERAL IDEA OF "PLAY DATES" TO BE VERY UNSETTLING.** All of these mothers of preschoolers driving themselves nuts trying to find new and endless ways to entertain their kids. I don't remember such a thing when I was growing up. It was left up to us to fend for ourselves and make our own friends at school or in our neighborhoods.

Not once do I recall my own mother getting out the roster of students from my class and going down the list to solicit a "play date" for me. That would be the day, right? But play dates are happening all over the place. Half the time the mother who would call me to set up a play date didn't even realize that my kid doesn't like her kid or vice versa. They just make the cold call and say, "Oh, Hi, my son/daughter is in your son'/daughter's class and he/she wants to invite him/her over for a play date." There's just something not right about getting two boys together and calling it a date of any kind if you ask me.

As if I didn't already have enough to do in my jam-packed day while my children were little, I had to add, "playdate" with so and so to the list. I always wondered what my son's reaction would be when I let him in on the plan for his social calendar. Once he actually said to me, "Oh my god Mom, why would you *ever* say I would go over there? I can't stand that kid! He trips me in the hallway practically every day." "Oh great," I thought to myself, "I just set up a date for my kid to get his ass kicked".

Occasionally it would work out well for everybody. When the kids got along and if they played well together it could actually turn out to be an indulgence for the mothers. If you got really lucky, after a few good "dates", you might actually have the opportunity to drop your kid off and run some errands.

How ironic that getting "lucky" after a few dates entailed the possibility of a trip to the grocery store alone? Being alone is a luxury after you have kids because it doesn't happen very often.

About the only shot I have of being alone now that I've had kids is when I'm in the shower. As a matter of fact, when I want to hide from my life its the first place I go. When everything all around me is falling apart, I just run for the shower. I lock the bathroom door, turn on the water and hide out. It's so peaceful in there, encapsulated in a refuge of warm steam and silence. I'm simply listening to the sound of the running water. It drowns out the screaming, the fighting, even the dog barking and the husband yelling.

It really doesn't even matter if I've already showered that day or not, I still find that it's the first place I head when things get out of control. Although most days I'm truly thrilled to get a shower any time before dinner, as I rarely get a chance in the morning. Mornings don't agree with me in general and I wish I could avoid them at all costs. Unfortunately my kids have to get up for school, which is a huge problem for somebody like me. Because of my great aversion to mornings, I pity anybody who has to see me before noon because, quite frankly, it's scary.

When my son was in preschool there was a day when I ran into one of those "Energizer Mommies", while she was dropping off *her* son. You know the type. She had a big happy grin waaaay too early in the morning and was practically skipping right toward me that ruinous day. I hadn't the faintest clue who she was until that day, but I instantly knew she was one of those freaks who wake up at the crack of dawn. She probably had to get up at least an hour or more before her kids, so she could get ready for her day. I, on the other hand, am usually woken up by the noise my kids generate by running through the house like elephants. Pitter-patter of little feet? Yeah. Right. As soon as my feet hit the floor I could be in the running as a top contestant for the "America's Most Frazzled Mom" competition—if such a thing really existed.

Freaks of nature like "Energizer Mommy" prepare for a preschool drop off the way most of us would get ready for a date. They are the moms who show up at 8 a.m. looking like they just stepped off the runway at a fashion show. What really blows my mind is that their makeup and hair are flawless so early in the morning. Their nails are done and they are wearing gorgeous outfits as though they have anywhere to actually go after preschool drop off.

All of that "perfection" must take them so much effort. I can't even imagine being that motivated. Then again, I *do* have a disability. The one that affects the part of my brain that is supposed to give a shit. It's tough enough just getting out the door at the crack of dawn, let alone coordinating lipstick and shoes. And to be honest, I just can't be bothered. Who do

I really need to impress anyway? I might say my husband but thankfully, he wouldn't notice if I dressed in garbage bags. I'm just the wife he loves. Fat, skinny, glamorous or frumpy, it's all the same to him.

That morning, when "Energizer Mommy" skipped over to me, it was at the normal preschool drop off time—8 a.m. And since 8 a.m. is long before the noon time hour, my hair was a mess and (dammit!) *of course* that was the morning I forgot my baseball cap. Thankfully, I had managed to throw on a pair of jeans. But the sweatshirt I was wearing had a huge bleach stain on it from having just sprayed Clorox Clean-Up around the bathroom after my son missed the bowl. I'm sure I hadn't looked in the mirror yet that day.

Even though I was afraid of what I might find, I yanked the rear view mirror down quickly to see if I would frighten myself. I looked like I had just been punched out with a couple of boxing gloves. Seeing the big black smudges under my eyes reminded me that I hadn't washed off my mascara from the night before.

I wondered what "Energizer Mommy" was thinking to herself about me that morning. She probably thought I was battling depression or got whacked in the face by my husband. I don't know what she thought but I do know that I looked like Hell. In case I hadn't mentioned it, I find it difficult to be social when I look like hell.

So there I was, dropping my son off at school, when Energizer Mommy ambushed me. "Oh, Hi there, I've been wanting to talk to you." she said with an unbearably wide, white smile. My name is Olivia. I'm Christopher's mom and you're Tommy's mom right? For a split second I didn't know how on earth she knew I was Tommy's mom, then I looked down and remembered he was attached to my hip. She buzzed like a bee and I couldn't help but envision a couple of batteries bolted into the bottom of her back.

I remembered I'd seen her early on a Monday morning once after she had chaired the "mother's tea" at school. I hadn't even made it to that event and guiltily, all I could think of was, "Oh God, please don't ask me where I was that morning!" I knew that she gave way too much time to organizing all the volunteer events for the school. I closed my eyes and prayed that she wouldn't ask me to volunteer for anything. I had already baked cookies for the bake sale and sold raffle tickets for the field trips! Wasn't that enough?

Much to my relief, she didn't ask me to volunteer for anything. However, she did want to know if we could set up a "play date". She also asked me for my address because she was planning her son's birthday party and wanted to invite my son. I managed to remember my address, not bad for that hour of the morning, so we talked about possible dates and times for a play date.

Later that same week the invitation to her son Christopher's birthday party arrived in the mail. I was impressed with myself for remembering to call Olivia to RSVP on time. Olivia and I ended up talking on the phone for quite a long time. I told her that Christopher's birthday party was going to be my son's first from his pre-school class and that we were excited to attend. That was actually a lie. My *son* was excited to go but I'd rather poke my eyes out with pencils any day of the week than attend yet another kid's birthday party.

About a week before the party I impressed myself further when I bought Christopher's birthday present a full *four days* ahead of time. I'm usually frantic the day before a party praying for a drive-thru CVS that will give me a kid's toy and wrap it to go. Wouldn't that be nice if they did?

The party fell near Thanksgiving, so it was also a really busy time of year. I'd wanted to make sure I could check everything off my list before the actual holiday. That particular weekend flew by and I remember that I wasn't particularly looking forward to going back to work on that Monday after Thanksgiving.

As I sat in the office checking my schedule and reviewing all the things I had to do at work, I just happened to glance at the Saturday block, which hit me like a brick in the stomach. I had completely forgotten all about Christopher's party! I'd never written it down in my personal calendar at home, just on my work schedule, which was a ridiculous thing to do because I wasn't even working that weekend.

What was I thinking? How could I have forgotten something that I was so prepared for? Where was my head? What was wrong with me? I had been way ahead of schedule, what happened? Jeez, I even had the present! I didn't know how I would ever face Olivia the "Energizer Mommy" again.

How could I call her and explain everything? At least if my son had been sick or if something else had come up at the last minute, I would have called her that morning. The party had totally slipped my mind so I never called, we just never showed up.

Maybe I could blame it on the tryptophan in the turkey or general holiday madness? At that point, I couldn't even bring myself to call her let alone think up excuses. I decided to let a few days pass and I prayed to God that I wouldn't run into her at school that week.

Eventually, I mustered up the nerve to call her and tried

my best to explain my mistake. When I get nervous, I babble uncontrollably. I can't shut up no matter how hard I try. I can't even think as fast as the stupid words are pouring out of my mouth. It's as if I'm a walking fire hydrant that has just been uncapped and I am overflowing with nonsense. I started disclosing all kinds of personal drama about my family and all the things that happened over Thanksgiving.

I guess in my warped mind, I figured if I came across as a total basket case, she would cut me some slack. Finally, she got a word in edgewise. I couldn't have been more relieved when she accepted my erratic apology and invited us over for a play date. There was that word again. Play date. I thought how strange it was that, after my snafu, she wanted our boys to have a play date. My son was still angry with me for missing the party but he got over it when I told him we were going over to Christopher's to play and he could bring the present to him then.

The big day arrived and we ventured over to their house. Not only was the house decorated extravagantly from top to bottom (of course!) but as always, when Olivia the "Energizer Mommy" answered the door she was dressed nicely enough to be going out on an *actual* date, not simply hosting a "play date".

As I suspected, we didn't have much in common but we made the best of it. I wasn't working that day and I had completed all of my Cinderella duties the previous day. I don't know how I did it but I somehow managed to take a shower before noon that day. I even took a few extra minutes to dry my hair and throw on a touch of make-up. I had a new sweater on and I dare say my confidence was about to take flight. Everything seemed to be going fine—Until the scream from hell echoed in our ears.

Both boys came flying down the stairs crying. Her son was

crying a lot louder than mine but together it was enough to warrant at least 1,000mg of Tylenol when I got home. We asked the boys what happened. Between sobs, they said they were fighting over a ball when her son said that my son bit him right in the arm. I gasped "Oh my god!" out loud and looked at my child in utter disbelief. "You have never bitten anybody in your life!" Well, except me, but that was when he was in the terrible two's and they didn't need to know that, did they? Still in shock I asked him, "Why did you do that?" He just kept crying while saying "He took the ball, he took the ball."

The degradation was unbearable and I could barely breathe. I quickly apologized, got my things grabbed my little pit bull and got out of there. I was still reeling inside about my son's actions long after the incident had ended. I couldn't believe he had done such a terrible thing. I remembered the times he had bitten me when he was a toddler and boy, did that hurt! Nothing quite like a couple of sharp teeth piercing your flesh to wake you up with a jolt first thing in the morning! And that was just normal baby biting behavior.

Sometimes people said I should bite him back when he did that, and although I thought it was funny, I could never imagine myself doing such a hurtful thing to my child. Thankfully, he outgrew that phase of his life but for some reason, that stage was back when I least expected it. And it was back to bite ME—right in the ass.

All I could think about then was that my kid was going to have a reputation as the animal that bites other kids. After the biting debacle, I thought for certain that my day couldn't possibly get any worse.

When I told my husband the story about what had happened

at the play date, he said, "Wow, that's too bad." Then he looked at me and asked, " You didn't wear your sweater like that did you?" I was dumbfounded. I just looked at him and said, "What are you talking about?" Then, as I looked down at my sweater, I saw that I had it on backwards.

With any other sweater, I might have been able to get away with it, but this particular sweater happened to have a little green horse in the top left corner. I had been wearing that sweater all day with the stupid green horse on my back under my right shoulder blade.

At that moment I thought, "Okay that settles it! If there is ever a contest to find 'America's most frazzled mom', I know I would win it, hands down. No doubt about it." *Especially if the judges knew, that on particularly fateful days, I wore my sweaters the same way I tended to live my life: Inside out and backwards.*

You're Screwed Mom

WHEN OUR CHILDREN WERE VERY YOUNG, my friend Chrissy and I established our amusing ritual of leaving each other voice mails pertaining to all the unimaginable things which had happened to us on a daily basis, essentially chronically "a day in the life of motherhood". We've been keeping up with our tradition for years, and one morning, when I got my daily distress call from Chrissy, I almost held my breath waiting to hear about her crisis du jour.

For several weeks, her youngest son Joey had been begging and pleading to go "inside" the coffee shop instead of just ordering at the drive-thru. Chrissy is somewhat of a fixture at the drive-thru line, ordering her "usual" at least three times a day but she's never been willing to knowingly set herself up for disaster by venturing inside the place with Joey.

She has spent so much time in the Heavenly Donuts drive-thru they named a specialty coffee after her. While this may sound like a joke, it's not. She ordered her signature daytime drink—French Vanilla iced coffee, two sweet and lows, skim milk with a touch of cream to lighten—on a daily basis so often that they created "The Chrissy Ice" in her honor. I thought she was kidding until I ordered it myself one day. Wonders never cease and sure enough, she was telling the truth about "The Chrissy Ice".

I hate to admit it, but I'm a little bit jealous of Chrissy's claim to fame. How many people do you know who have a drink named after them? I know it doesn't seem like much but in our world of kids, laundry, work, playdates and more laundry? Believe me, it's huge.

Like everything else in our chaotic world, Chrissy's claim to fame didn't come without a price. After suffering through as many days of whining as is humanly possible, Joey's desire to actually enter Heavenly Donuts eventually wore Chrissy down. The day of reckoning had finally come when she could no longer suppress Joey's cries. And reckon she did.

It was time for the unthinkable and she knew it. She donned the best mom armor she could muster and marched forward into Heavenly Donuts with pride. The place was brimming with customers (mostly elderly of course) and nearly every seat was filled. Somehow, Chrissy had managed to find an open booth. It was claustrophobic and small but it would have to do as they sat down for their mother/son breakfast date.

Chrissy looked at her watch and was surprised to discover that they had been there for a full five minutes and Joey hadn't wreaked any havoc yet. Just when she allowed herself to drift into these semi pleasant thoughts, the frightening culmination of what she had set herself up for was about to take place. Joey asked her, with a worried expression on his face, "Mom, what's that going Bzzzz, Bzzzz?" Despite Chrissy's peerless efforts to explain to him there was no buzzing sound, he was adamant that he heard buzzing and she could not convince him otherwise. Joey has an intense fear of bees. If anything even slightly resembles the sound of a bee buzzing, he's guaranteed to flip his lid. Chrissy felt her stomach knot up thinking, "Dear lord, what is this kid gonna do now?"

Unpredictability hovered at the core of Joey's nature. He might accidentally scald her with coffee, by throwing her cup into the air. Or he might whip his sticky donut at some unsuspecting ninety-year-old person's head.

As she continued to argue with him against his notion that there was a bee somewhere, it became alarmingly quiet in the donut shop. It was either that or Chrissy was *hallucinating* the quiet, because her mother's intuition had kicked in to warn her that all holy hell was about to break loose. She sensed that she was sitting right inside the "calm before the storm". Seeing the look on Joey's face she braced herself for the impending blow-up.

Sure enough, in seconds, Joey screamed like he had a giant bullhorn to his lips, "Mom, I am telling you right now if you're wrong, and that is a bee in here, you are screwed!" All she heard was screwed, screwed, screwed, mom you are screwed, over and over echoing through her head.

Every last sweet, frail, elderly person turned around and stared at her in disgrace. All she could do was blankly stare back at them, unable to make any apologies, shameful or otherwise. She dragged her unmindful child out of there by his coat sleeve and never looked back.

She felt the stare of many pairs of old eyes on her, as she thought to herself, "Sure, sit there and judge me. I know back in your day, you would've yanked him out by his ear and had him home over your knee with a belt across his ass in two minutes flat." Of course these days, if you so much as give your kid a flinger flick, someone calls The Department of Social Services to investigate.

So, because we can no longer legally beat our kids within an inch of their lives, as was the socially acceptable norm about fifty or so years ago, we have to resort to *other* coping mechanisms. Like anti-depressants. And wine.

A friend of mine once confided, "I'm telling you, every single damn night when I leave work and climb into my car, I have to fight with myself to get onto 95 north and head home. Because all I really wanna do is drive 100mph toward 95 South and keep going until I hit the Mexican border. Sometimes, I really dread 5:00p.m. It sucks to leave my paying job to go home to *another* job that pays you nothing but expects you to give the world and beyond."

I don't know what kind of reaction she expected from me after her candid disclosure, but I asked her if she knew where I could buy a sombrero 'cause I was definitely riding shotgun, if and when, she ever hits the road and heads South.

My Mom is 64!

ONE NEVER KNOWS WHAT WILL COME OUT OF THE MOUTHS OF BABES, but one thing is for certain, it's almost always a shocker. Once when I had to pick up my daughter and her friend Lilly from Kindergarten, I got quite an earful. As I neared the pick up area, the two little girls came into view. There they were, the two little angels, standing on the curb with their teacher. "How cute are they?" I thought to myself, as I pulled up, and helped them into the car.

They were so precious at that age. They were still babies in some ways, yet at the same time, starting to blossom into little girls. I loved to listen to them talk, because even though they would try their best to sound all grown up, I could still detect the baby talk behind their new "big girl" words.

It was a good thing I loved listening to them talk, because even now that she's older, my little girl never stops talking. I can't say I don't know where she gets it from, as she's probably a fourth generation flapper. It could be more, although currently, that's as far back as I've been able to trace it. She talks day and night; she's even been known to talk *while* she's sleeping. As I pulled out of the parking lot that particular day, she excitedly said to her friend, "Did I tell you what Jimmy did the other day?" Jimmy is a neighbor's little brother. She went over there to play and got lucky enough to catch him running around naked. This was a huge event in her week, and she told anybody who would listen. The way she went on about it, you might not think she has a brother of her own. Apparently, it's way funnier when it's somebody else's brother. "Yes I know what Jimmy did, you already told me you saw his butt crack!" Lilly giggled. I was laughing to myself, while I scolded them for using the word "butt crack", and kindly asked them to change the subject.

As the old saying goes, "Be careful what you wish for." The subject changed all right and it was no longer about butt cracks. Suddenly, the conversation had shifted to wieners. My daughter couldn't seem to get the words out fast enough as she said, "I know I told you about that, but did I tell you I saw his wiener?" With this admission, they both broke into a fit of giggles. I was about to reprimand them, when Lilly came out with, "Oh it's not that big of a deal, and I've seen wieners before. Big ones too, like my brother's, and my father's and even my mother's." I almost drove off the road when that one came out.

Despite my best mothering efforts, I laughed out loud, as I tried to erase the visual of Lilly's all too feminine mom suddenly sporting a big wiener under her skirt. Once I caught my breath, I told them that they needed to respect other people's privacy and not talk about stuff like that.

My face may have been dead serious but I was roaring on the inside. When I told my husband what happened, he asked if I planned to tell Lilly's mom that I knew she had a wiener. I laughed, but in the end, I opted to keep that bit of information to myself. Who knows how she would have reacted to something like that? Not everybody has the same warped sense of humor that my husband and I share. I'm sure my daughter has said many things to other parents that I wouldn't care to know about. I would love to be a fly on the wall in their classroom with all of the things they come out with sometimes.

One year I attended a Mother's Day show presented by my son's class when he was in Elementary School. I was astounded at the amount of dirty laundry those seven year olds aired. There they were, all standing in a row, first graders holding up poster sized pictures they had drawn of their moms. On the back of the posters were some things they had to say about their mothers.

The first thing I noticed on my son's portrait of me was that I had a huge smile on my face. "That's a positive," I thought. "At least he sees me as happy right?" He has always been a talented artist and overall, it was a fairly good depiction of me. Quite possibly, it was *too* good. When I looked closely at my hair in the picture, it was brown. Then I noticed he had colored in all black under the brown, delineating the roots. Wow, what a wake up call that was! I guess if seeing that didn't get me to my hairdresser immediately for a touch up, nothing ever will.

Every kid in the room had an opportunity to get up in front of the audience of mothers and in their own words, disclose a few adorable little anecdotes to describe how they saw their mothers in daily life. It went something like this: "My mom is 36 years old...My mom is nice because...My mom likes to... My mom's favorite food is...I love my mom because..." I know I wasn't alone as I held my breath and waited for my son's big moment. As each child stood up and recited stories about their mothers, you could feel the tension in the room growing thicker.

All the moms were collectively feeling each other's pain. One kid said, "My mom is 64 years old." Another said, "My mom is nice because she only yells sometimes." There were comments like, "My mom likes to talk on the phone all day." And, "My mom's favorite food is cheesecake." I remember looking over at the mom who, according to her child, was supposedly sixty-four and she couldn't have been a day over thirty. She didn't look thrilled about being called sixty-four. Although the mom sitting next to her was positively elated when her child professed her to be twenty-two when she was easily *at least* forty-two.

We all laughed at these silly declarations and got a kick out of how our children saw us. Though deep down, we were all terrified of the ugly truth spilling out of the mouths of babes. The longer I had to wait for my son's turn, the more my anxiety grew. "What was my son gonna say about me? Was he gonna rat me out for waking up late every day? Would he say I was fifty years old? That's definitely how old I felt at the time. Would he tell all of the other moms that, while I didn't have a favorite food, I liked to drink red wine?

I thought about causing my cell phone to go off so I could run out of there, hoping it'd get him, and me, off the hook. But as petrified as I was of the truth, I stuck it out. Thankfully my son didn't say anything I found humiliating. I was overcome with relief when our "Mother's Day" at school was over.

Kids can't help their brutal honesty. They haven't yet learned the art of censorship and tact. My daughter once asked me, "Mommy do you have a baby in your butt?" My friend's little boy, when he was two years old, asked his mom why didn't she have a fire hose like daddy? My son once called Santa on a cable television show from his grandmother's house. When Santa asked him what he wanted for Christmas, He replied, "I'm all set Santa, but would you PLEASE bring those kid's in Africa some food so that my grandma will stop making me eat green beans?" I have another friend who once took her five-year old to his doctor for his annual check-up and when the doctor examined him, realized he had to suction out her son's nose. After the doctor finished, her little boy looked at him and said, "Wow, that really sucked!" My friend gasped thinking her child was saying something potentially horrific, was completely caught off guard when the doctor explained to her that her child was talking about the nose-suction device. Her son had meant the word both literally and as it turned out, appropriately.

I think due to our experiences with our children's "honestly", we expect the worst to come out. We try to prepare for whatever will mortify us the most and are surprised, more often than not, when it isn't as bad as we imagined it would be. As parents, not only do we have to worry about what might come out of their mouths, but we also face equal fear for what might come out due to their lack of impulse control.

When my son was very young, he once poured an entire cup of Coke right down the back of my father's pants. There was my poor, unsuspecting father innocently bending over to fix something, which my son used as a fine opportunity to try a new experiment on his Papa. He saw a little bit too much of his Papa's backside exposed, which apparently, as far as my son was concerned, looked like a great place to pour a nice, cold, fizzy drink. Why wouldn't pouring a little coke into Papa's "butt crack" (to use the proper terminology my children have taught me) seem like fun to a three-year-old? What a sticky situation that must have been for my dad–especially toward the end of the day!

There are definitely times when I wish I could live my life the way a three-year-old does. Oh the pure joy of doing whatever my heart desired in any given moment! It must be a blast! How many times would *I* have absolutely loved to pour an icy cold coke down somebody's pants? For the hell of it mind you, not necessarily because they actually pissed me off.

There was one summer when some of my friends, with our kids in tow, took a day trip up to our friend Jenn's cabin on Lake Winnipesaukee. I should have known the day was going to be an absolute horror show when, within the first ten minutes of arrival, all of our boys came across a dead chipmunk floating in a bucket of water. Of course, being curious young boys, they wouldn't leave it alone. Why wouldn't they be completely enthralled with such a sight?

Proving my point about children and their lack of impulse control, they all hovered around that bucket of dirty water and couldn't control themselves from relentlessly poking and prodding that poor, dead chipmunk.

Once the fascination with the dead rodent ended, they went on to other mischievous adventures. The kids could hardly contain themselves when they saw the golf cart Jenn and her family use to drive down to the beach. The golf cart could only hold a few people at a time, but of course, they all wanted to ride in it simultaneously. We were all going to go down to the beach, so we had to divide up the group for the multiple trips it would take to get everyone there. And so, the wars began.

The kids all fought about who was going to go first, who was going to go with whom and where they were going to sit. Why can't anything with kids ever be easy? How could we have thought we were actually going to have a fun and relaxing time when we drove up to the lake for the day? On second thought, maybe we only *dreamed* about it being fun.

On some level, I think we all knew our day wasn't going to be relaxing. Not by any stretch of the imagination. Somehow, three or four trips in the golf cart later, we'd managed to get down to the beach somewhat successfully. Shockingly, nobody had to pee.

We spotted a group of teenagers staking out their territory on a raft in the middle of the lake. We watched, as the teenagers lit up cigarettes, while our tribe of unruly eight-year-olds swam vigorously toward the same raft to claim what they felt were their rightful spots. The situation had disaster written all over it.

As the day unfolded, it seemed like the insanity was going to keep getting better and better. If we managed to return home with the same number of people we left with, it would be a miracle. After we'd gotten everyone settled, we'd attempted to take a few moments to relax as much as we could, given our circumstances.

We stared in envy at a group of young, single, childless people lounging on the beach. They were drinking beer, playing cards, listening to music and seemed to be having a fantastic time. I was lost in that moment of time, desperately trying to remember the last time *I* had been able to sit on a beach drinking beers, listening to music, without having to chase kids around while trying to sunblock their nose for the nine millionth time.

Before I could start getting additionally depressed over things like the last time I wore a bikini or how luxurious it would feel to sprawl out on a towel and actually close my eyes, my little reverie was ended abruptly. It was time for lunch, which meant it was time to gather up our maniacs and start the next round of "Golf Cart Wars".

On our way back to Jenn's cabin, the sky grew black. Rain started moving in, so we quickened our pace. We were running around grabbing towels, chairs, and all of our kid's stuff. Jenn made a fast trek up to her cabin in the golf cart to unload all of our beach gear. She quickly returned to park the golf cart close by while we all hurried to grab the rest of our things. The first drops of rain began to fall and in the blink of an eye, Chrissy's son Joey jumped in the cart and took over the driver's seat.

We all know Joey. While all kids are somewhat unpredictable, he is The King. As soon as we saw him sit down, we asked Jenn if the key was in the ignition. She said, "Oh don't worry, he can't start it." Chrissy and I knew in an instant that no matter what Jenn said, Joey would, somehow, be able to start that cart and he'd be cruising in less than a millisecond. She looked at me, I looked at her and before we could even jump, Joey had that cart on the move! By that time, all of the kids were piled aboard that thing. If Joey was driving, they were riding. Immediately, Chrissy and I sprang into action and I don't think my heart had ever pounded so fast!

While trying to warn all of the innocent bystanders, we screamed out at them to take cover. Panic set in and I was frozen with fear. All I could see was a blur, which I knew was Jenn running. She ran so fast, I swear she had to be airborne. She landed in the cart on top of Joey, just as it crashed into an empty picnic table. Thank God that picnic table was there, because all I could imagine was that golf cart full of kids heading straight into the water.

We later discovered that there was a flip switch for the ignition but Jenn never thought Joey would figure it out so quickly. Being Joey, of course he figured it out, before she could even finish her sentence. We all had to promise not to tell the Daddies what happened at the lake that day. Sorta like, "What happens in Vegas stays in Vegas" but not even half as thrilling. Jenn said that if her husband ever found out what happened, he would be furious, and would never let the kids on the golf cart again. The things we mothers do to protect our children! At times, even from their fathers.

Ah Motherhood! We give it everything we have, yet what do we get in return? A portrait of our very bad roots held up in front of a class full of people for Mother's Day, that's what.

I suppose it's all relative though, because as soon as we think we've got it bad, we hear about some other pitiful mother who has it infinitely worse. Like that poor mom out there who has a big wiener.

Recliners on Mars

IN MY OPINION, "THE RECLINER" IS BY FAR THE WORST INVENTION IN THE WORLD. I want to sue the person who invented this useless and hideous piece of furniture. Forget about going after the tobacco industry for hooking hundreds of millions on cigarettes—I want to go after the furniture companies. They've somehow managed to create a product that has not only turned my husband into a TV and chair addict, but has caused him to be so disabled by it, that he can't get off his ass to help me. Recliners should come with a warning: Use of this product may cause excessive laziness, wife specific deafness, and uncontrollable bodily gas and scratching.

The only thing worse than that damn recliner is ESPN. Sometimes I think we should build an in-law apartment onto our house. Not for my actual in-laws though—for me. When I come home from work, hear the TV blaring, see my husband sitting there in that recliner all sprawled out and comfy-cozy watching his daily updates—I just wanna scream.

I do admit that my husband is far better than most husbands.

The truth is, he does actually help me out around the house a lot. I just get so frustrated when I come home from work and get out of my car knowing that it will be the last time I sit down until the next day when I get back into my car to drive the kids to school.

I wouldn't have the faintest idea how it feels to walk in the door after a long day at work and sit down in a chair. As silly as it sounds, I actually look forward to getting a cold so that I can wrap up in a blanket on the couch and do nothing.

For Mother's Day one year, I asked to sit in daddy's recliner for the day. It seems unfair that like me, so many women in the world go through life feeling guilty when or if we simply sit down long enough to catch our breath. I could never relax in any kind of chair if I knew there were dishes in the sink or clutter all over the counters. Yet, I have walked into my own house on many occasions and seen my husband doing just that. It doesn't bother him in the least. His excuse is, that even if he picked up all the mess it wouldn't matter, because the kids would have it upside down again by the time he sat back down.

I have to say there is *some* truth to his point but still, how is it so easy for him to relax and ignore it? I know my husband isn't alone in this. I have walked into so many of my friends' homes when they weren't there and found their husbands just sitting in their recliners glued to the television, while the house looked like a bomb had just exploded.

Is it just that watching sports on TV is so distracting that these men can't see the crap all around them? Or is it that they really couldn't care less? How is it that when *their* friends come over, they don't give a damn if the house is a pigsty? How can they just crack open the beers and shoot the shit despite dirty laundry all over the floor, crumbs on the counter, toys everywhere? How can they do that? HOW? If anybody knows the secret, I want to know because I'm tired of carrying the burden on my shoulders all the time.

I have become so overwhelmed with carrying what feels like the weight of the world, that I feel like hanging a huge "Quarantine" sign on my door so that everybody will stay away. There are days when I honestly can't stand the idea of another day of housework. Talk about monotony! Day in and day out it's always the same. I know a lot of people say that it's a beautiful thing to have toys everywhere, that it's a sign of a happy, healthy house. But those people are *grandparents*. I wish husbands would posses a little bit of the mommy guilt and want to pick things up due to the fear of humiliation from unexpected guests.

What is even more disconcerting than a man turning into an actual La-Z-Boy, (I guess they really weren't joking around when they came up with that name) is the way that I've heard these same husbands distort the reality of their lives in public.

I once heard my friend's husband professing his exceptional house cleaning skills to the parents of children on an entire little league team. The only thing he left out in his version of the truth was the French Maid outfit and feather duster. Even worse was the fact that his wife was home with the flu and there he was, obnoxiously bragging to all of the other parents about how he had woken up at the crack of dawn to wash all the laundry and dishes. As if he was doing her a huge favor instead of merely doing his part. Meanwhile, his pathetic wife was deathly sick in bed. Laundry and dishes were *the very least* he could do!

Actually, his wife was lucky she didn't have to hear him spouting off. If I had to hazard a guess, there is a strong probability that she would prefer to be smothered by a pillow than have to listen to her husband sling his bullshit.

I called my friend the next day after hearing her husband boast about being "The Husband and Father of the Year", to find out if she was feeling better. She was strong enough to stand, which to her husband, meant she'd made a full recovery. Sure enough, her husband had rushed back to work now that, in his mind, his wife was absolutely fine. And as a thoughtful parting gift, he'd left her a sink full of disgustingly dirty dishes.

The rice had stuck to the plates so hard she had to soak them for hours just to be able to wash them. There were food crumbs scattered under the dining room table, finger paint and clay were splattered everywhere in the kitchen. Oh sure, it was great that daddy had let the kids' paint and use modeling clay, but did he clean it up? Of course he didn't. But at the same time that rice was hardening onto the dishes and finger paint was drying on the ceilings, he had no problem nominating himself for the husband and father of the year award to the little league team parents, now did he?

I realize that not all husbands are created equal. I know there are a lot of them out there that do a tremendous amount, even some who gladly do more of the housework than their wives. However, I doubt this is the case with most. More than likely, I'd say the majority of wives are dealing with the same issues of clueless husbands and I would like to add, that I for one, will continue to hold the recliner responsible as a big culprit in the current crisis.

How funny would it be to call the furniture company requesting to return their recliners by asking company employees to show up in person to haul it out of your house? I wonder what their reaction would be when stating that the reason for the return was: "because my husband got his ass stuck in it." I'd love nothing more than to tell those people to take the stupid thing out of my home and never bring it back again.

Since I'm on a roll here with the husband bashing, another thing that really annoys me is when they make stuff up purely for the sake of making it up. I don't really have this one quite figured out yet but I'm leaning toward the idea of general laziness. Most of the annoying things men do usually stems from laziness if you really think about it.

The "making stuff up" comes into play in all types of situations. On more than one occasion, my husband has answered a phone call from one of my friends when I wasn't home. I don't, for the life of me, know why he doesn't just let the call go to voicemail? It definitely seems like answering the phone is far too much work for him. I also don't know why, when he actually does decide to pick up the phone and open his mouth to talk, he can't just tell the truth? Usually my friends will ask if I'm home and instead of saying, "No she isn't here, can I take a message?" he just makes up whatever comes into his mind at that moment.

He will say absolutely anything that he feels like saying, for no other reason that I can think of, than to just "make stuff up". He has told my friends that I'm at the mall shopping when I'm actually at work. He has said I was at work when I was getting my hair done. He has said that I was sleeping when I was in the shower. I don't know why he does it, but he does. It's one of those mysteries of the husband that I have yet to discern.

Maybe it is really just a man thing because I remember my own father doing this when I was young too. So many times,

I'd make plans with a friend and as soon as they'd call, my dad would say I'd left for the day, when I was really in the shower getting ready. He got me in a lot of trouble with that. I have no idea why they do it (but they definitely do) and it's just plain weird if you ask me.

Years ago, there was a school fundraiser I attended with my husband and kids. My friend Sue was supposed to be there as well but she had to take one of her kids to a birthday party that night. She didn't want her other child to miss the special night, so she had asked her husband to step up and take him to the event. The fundraiser was an Art Show and it turned out to be a great night, especially when we saw the extravagant gifts they had to raffle off. We all put our names in hoppers to try and win themed baskets made up by our kids' classes.

One of the baskets made every mother in the room positively drool. It was a "Mom's Pampering Basket", filled with lavish items like citrus & lemon energy scrub, lavender bubble bath, a pedicure kit and a gift certificate to a local day spa. I can assure you that every mother in that room wanted to win that basket, myself included.

The only thing that has even come remotely close to exciting me as much as the idea of winning that basket, was the day I found a hole at the bottom of my silverware drawer. I happily stumbled upon five year's worth of lost silverware that had fallen through the abyss down into a lower drawer. I jumped up and down in my kitchen, danced around and screamed with delight when I saw my old veggie peeler and pie servers galore. How many thanksgivings had passed and I'd had to cut pie with a knife?

It scared me a little knowing how excited I got over something so trivial—but it scared my friend, Mindy, more. She was sitting there when I found the formerly lost silverware and I watched her facial expression change from confusion, to embarrassment, to pure pity as she saw my reaction to finding lost silverware. Surely I needed to win that pampering basket if finding missing pie servers gave me so much joy. Sue's husband had actually put a ticket into the pampering basket to try and win it for her and lo and behold, well wouldn't you know? They pulled out her name!

Of course I shed a little tear when they didn't call *my* name but if it couldn't be me who won the basket, I was elated that it was Sue. She deserved it as much as the rest of us, if not more. She busts her ass day in and day out. She juggles a full time job as an Esthetician, while raising two kids, and taking care of aging parents. She runs a mommy marathon every single day and yet, she never stops. Not even for a second.

Mothers all over the room united the night of the fundraiser and applauded for her when she won that basket. Despite the fact that she wasn't there, we all had a sweet little tribute in her honor. I knew that like many husbands, Sue's didn't always give her credit where credit was due, so I went a little overboard stressing how much she deserved to win the pampering basket, especially the trip to the spa. I rambled on about her qualifications to hold court as mother of the year, how she does it all with finesse and makes it look easy when we ALL know it isn't.

Of course, when her husband actually brought home the basket and gave it to her, it was a totally different story. He mentioned *none* of the praises we all sung in her name, choosing instead to tell her that the rest of us were all fuming and jealous that *our* husbands didn't win it for us. He stole the glory of the evening, omitted our heartfelt tribute and declared himself a big fat hero. I couldn't believe it! I suppose it just goes to show that these men really do live on Mars.

I've never even read the "Mars and Venus" book but there's gotta be something to it. It definitely seems like men and women are from two totally different planets, even if it's not Mars and Venus. If it *is* Mars and Venus, I'm convinced that on Mars there's nothing more than millions of recliners, lots of beer, unrestrained gas, and full blast ESPN 24/7.

The Curse of the Necklace

I LOVE TO WATCH MY CHILDREN SLEEP. They always look so peaceful and angelic. And boy oh boy, do I ever dread dragging them out of their warm cozy beds early in the morning to get them up and ready for school. As a result, Mondays are pretty awful in general. However, some Mondays are an extra special kind of awful. Particularly when the alarm doesn't go off and it throws off the entire day.

I remember one such Monday, many years ago, when the alarm never went off and we all overslept. I opened my eyes and stared in denial at the clock on my bedside table. It was three minutes before eight o'clock, which was precisely the time I knew the bus would be pulling up to our stop. I couldn't believe I had slept that late. I knew there was going to be hell to pay once my son found out he wouldn't be able to make the bus. He has always been superstitious and he tells me all the time that if he starts out his day badly, (like missing the bus), the rest of the day will be cursed.

Sure enough, when I went into his room to wake him up and

he saw the time, he was understandably irate with me. If there is one thing he hates more than anything it is being driven to school by his mother.

I made a sad attempt at an apology but it wasn't flying. We both knew he wouldn't be forgiving me anytime soon. I made his lunch in record time and got my daughter up and dressed as well. She would need to be dropped at pre-school right after I delivered my son to school on time.

The entire way to school he was spouting his mouth off about how he was gonna be late and everybody was gonna pick on him. This kid has always been such a worrywart. I kept telling him that school didn't officially start until 8:45a.m. And it wasn't even 8:20 a.m. yet. I may as well have been talking to the dashboard because he was hearing none of it. His mouth didn't stop for a minute. He went on and on and on, never letting up, not even to take a breath.

I tuned him out, as I always do, although that morning I did happen to catch a glimpse of him in the rear view mirror. I was surprised to see him wearing an obnoxious gold necklace I'd never seen before. It looked like something that Mr. T would wear. It was gigantic around his neck and he looked ridiculous.

Leave it to me to upset the applecart even more by asking him to take it off. Angrily, he told me that the necklace was cool. I abandoned the subject at that point, because what did I really know about what was cool? It felt like it had been hundreds of years since I'd been in third grade. I don't even think he waited for me to put the car in park before he practically dove out into the parking lot and took off as fast as he could. I drove off exasperated, thinking to myself, "God, the kids at school will probably ask him if he's got any drugs or ladies for sale looking the way he does with that gold chain."

A few minutes after dropping off my little "gangsta", I pulled up to my daughter's school, where we had to drive up and meet the teachers instead of just letting our kids dive out of the car headfirst.

By the time we arrived she was late too, of course, but she was three years old then and it was a good thing (for me) she didn't have any time skills yet. As I stopped the car, it felt like midnight already. Had the day really only just begun? I helped her out of her car seat and looked around for her backpack. Naturally, it was nowhere to be found. I had left it at home hanging by the door. Big surprise the way the day was going! I needed to think quickly and find something, *anything*, for her to carry her work home in. I jumped out of the car, whipped the doors open and frantically searched for anything that slightly resembled a bag.

As I rummaged through toys, trash and all sorts of lovely pre-school artwork creations, I spotted my pink and blue canvas tote bag wedged between the seat and the floor. It was stuck and I had to give it several good yanks before it broke free and sent me flying almost out the door and onto the pavement.

When I saw the pink ribbon on the side of the bag, I suffered a momentary surge of guilt. This was the bag I had bought to benefit breast cancer research, yet here it was, stuck under my seat among the goldfish crackers and gummy worms. By that time, I was in a sweat and my nerves were shot. I grabbed the bag and my daughter as I saw her teacher coming up the walkway. I doubt if her sweet and patient teacher would have even given a damn that I forgot my daughter's backpack but somehow, I felt the need to justify my carelessness.

I handed my smiling daughter off to Mrs. M., grabbed the pink and blue tote and handed that off to her as well. Then I unleashed a big, long, crazy explanation, as only I can, which nobody but me cares about. I could hear myself saying to the teacher, "Oh, it was such a chaotic morning! We woke up late, my son missed the bus, we were running out the door and I'm so sorry I forgot her Hello Kitty Backpack! By the way, she doesn't even have her snack; I could run home and get her one? I'm really so sorry about the backpack, Mrs. M. but, I do have this lovely breastfeeding bag." I instantly realized what I had said, and although Mrs. M.'s lips were moving, I was too overcome with my own thoughts to hear what she was saying.

All I could think was, "Oh my god, did I just say I had a breastfeeding bag? I didn't just say that, did I? My youngest child is in her class, she is three, please no, please god, I didn't just say that I had a breastfeeding bag." But I did say it, I knew I did and there wasn't anything I could say now to retract it. Even though she was almost to the door of the school, I was still rambling in a pathetic attempt at an explanation to her back (as if she even cared) and she just kept right on walking.

Later that day when my daughter came home from school, I checked the infamous "breastfeeding bag". She had colored some beautiful butterflies, ladybugs, made some watercolor paintings and even formed a perfect letter S. As I was going through all of her things, I happened to notice a stray tampon in the little inside pocket of the bag. Nothing like sending my three year old to school with a tampon AND a breastfeeding bag.

A bit later, when my son got off his bus he was sporting the "I-had-a-crappy-day-don't-come-near-me" face. I thought overall, it was better not to ask. As we walked down the street to our house he took it upon himself to start ranting and raving about what a bad day he had. He said, "It's all your fault mom! YOU overslept! YOU made me miss the stupid bus and then YOU cursed my necklace. It's ALL YOUR FAULT!" He told me that he had gotten in trouble for talking at lunch and again on the playground for chasing after a runaway football and then some kids called him a girl for wearing the necklace.

I didn't bother to ask him exactly how "I" had cursed the necklace, but I figured it must have been from my oversleeping, because after all, wasn't *I* the one who suggested he might want to take off that necklace in the first place? Oh well, I figured no point in arguing with him because I haven't won one yet. I just shouldered the blame like a good mom and let it go. Lucky for me, he said he was never wearing that necklace again.

I thought about my day and all of the things that had happened. Maybe my son really did have a point? I've always heard people say when you wake up on the wrong side of the bed and stub your toe, you know it's gonna be "one of those days."

I guess I would have to say in this case, that theory proved true. Gold chains, tampons and breastfeeding bags...Oh my!

Pancakes aren't just for Breakfast

LIKE MANY OF MY OTHER MOTHERS IN ARMS, I have had the distinct pleasure of being at Chuck E Cheese for a variety of children's birthday parties. There is nothing quite like the feeling of being in a hot, sweaty room full of hundreds of screaming kids, loud arcade games and blinking lights. The only saving grace about that place is that they serve wine. Oh yeah, they also stamp your hands and your kid's hands with matching numbers to keep track of who belongs to whom. They also have a pretty good security system, so nobody can escape the building even if they want to. Not even mothers.

On one particular afternoon at Chuck E. Cheese the kids were packed in the place like sardines. Of course they were! It was a Saturday afternoon birthday party.

I instantly hated the mother who had planned a stupid birthday party at Chuck E. Cheese on a Saturday. Yeah, I know people have to work, kids have school and life during the week can get busy but couldn't she have simply thrown a nice *family* party at her home? That would have saved us all a lot of aggravation.

So there we were, my friends and I, with all of our kids at yet another nerve-grating birthday party. It was just one more warm, sunny Saturday afternoon cooped up in germville.

Ninety minutes is about the standard time for a party at upchuck cheese and we usually start counting down after the first sixty. Things were going along status quo, the pizza was done, the cake was done and the presents were opened. The kids had all danced with Chuck E. and cashed in their tickets. The only thing left before we could get the heck out of dodge, was distribution of the goody bags.

Every parent knows that no kid will leave a party until they get their goody bag. It's hard enough to drag them out anyway, so why prolong the torture? I remember standing there while thinking, "Come on already! Give out the damn bags! It's time to GO!" As we waited impatiently for the goody bags, all the kids ran back up to the tunnel tubes.

There isn't enough Lysol or Clorox in the world to clean those tubes. There were so many kids in there at once that every time one would come out, they were sopping with sweat. I was contemplating how I could ever possibly get the shower water hot enough to disinfect my kids when one of the sweaty tube monsters came out screaming, "Somebody pooped up there mom!" Every mother there looked at each other and exchanged disgusted glances.

Most of our kids were already potty trained but Chrissy's son, Joey, still had occasional accidents. She looked over at me while she pleaded, "Oh, please god, not Joey." I tried my best to reassure her saying, "Don't worry! What are the chances it's Joey? There are a billion kids in there." I hadn't even gotten the sentence out, when Chrissy's son Mark came tumbling out of the bottom of the tube and yelled, "Mommmm! I think Joey pooped up there and everybody is climbing through it." She took off running in a manic search for her youngest child and much to her despair, when she looked up, she could see Joey was way up at the top of the tubes.

Chrissy reluctantly climbed in and sure enough, as she reached midway, there it was: a giant brown mashed pancake. The smell was enough to gag her, as she uttered all kinds of profanities, under her breath. She still wasn't sure if it was actually her kid who was the guilty party pooper but no matter what, she had to find Joey, and find him fast! She furiously climbed through the remainder of the maze.

With her knees burning, her back aching, and sweat profusely dripping from her forehead, she forged ahead. She was determined to find her child at all costs. She finally spotted him once she'd reached the top of the tubes. With what little strength she had left, she struggled to grab Joey, and drag him out of there.

When they both reached the bottom and had safely climbed out of the crazed maze, the first thing Chrissy did, was what any good mother in her situation would have done: She buried her nose in his butt, and took a giant sniff. "Dammit" she said miserably looking at the rest of us. "He does stink, he must have done it!" All the moms rallied for Chrissy, as we hurried to grab napkins for her. We even wet some with water under the soda fountain. We all felt terribly for her but none of us felt quite badly enough to go into the trenches to help her clean it up. Back into the tubes she went.

Once again, she was crawling through the tunnels, scrunched over, with burning knees, an aching back and sweating like a pig while she searched for "the pancake". While she was in there doing what she had to do, I kept her child glued to my side. I figured it was the least I could do, since there was no way in hell I was going up there with her. During the time I was waiting with him, Joey innocently looked up at me and said, "I didn't do that poopy up there you know, I just had a little gas." I was not surprised when he used the word "gas" because I knew Chrissy's rule about not saying the word "fart". I asked him, "Why didn't you tell your mommy that when she dragged you out" He said, "She didn't ask me."

All I could think of was, "Can I get to her before she gets to the pancake?" Wait until she found out it wasn't Joey's "accident". Heaven help her if she was already there. Chrissy has always been a paranoid germophobe as it is, so I could only imagine what she would do when she found out it wasn't *HER* kid's pancake.

Just as I was deliberating whether or not to go up to get her, another mom had managed to wrangle one of the employees. He was headed our way, with a spray bottle of bleach and paper towels. I couldn't help but think to myself, "Wow, I'd hate to have his job." I thought about telling his boss to give him a raise after this nightmare.

I felt like I was in slow motion while I heard my own screams echoing in my ears yelling, "Chrissy, Noooooo!" I was so afraid she wouldn't hear me but I caught a glimpse of her looking down at me through one of the giant bubbles overhead. She understood my frantic attempt at sign language when I pointed to Joey's butt and shook my head "no"! Meanwhile that pitiful employee had to go up there and quite literally do the dirty work.

Just as Chrissy was making her way out of the maze, the little boy who dropped the infamous "pancake", was overheard telling his mother that he'd had an accident up there, and that he was sorry he couldn't hold it. If only he'd admitted to it earlier, he could have saved Chrissy from a lot of unnecessary torture.

Chuck E.'s closed the maze down, which hopefully meant they were fumigating the whole thing. After the poop mania died down, we eventually received the goody bags and got out of there as fast as our little legs would carry us.

I'm sure we all must have scrubbed our kids with Brillo pads and Clorox that night. Having experienced that lovely little nightmare, I definitely think Chuck E. Cheese needs a better wine list. Maybe even a martini bar.

The Family Jewels

I THINK EVERY MOTHER IN THE WORLD CAN RELATE TO FEELING HER CHILD'S PAIN. It is the worst feeling in the world to see your child get hurt and we would do anything to take away their boo-boos. About the only thing we can usually offer is a little TLC. We are the ones there to wash it up, put on the Neosporin ointment and bandages, and finish it off with a big hug and kiss. I, like every other mother have done this on countless occasions. Especially being the mother of a super active little boy. He has been hurt more times than I will ever be able to count.

When he was little he actually had a black and blue mark on his head for an entire year. It wasn't the same one, he just kept hitting his head over and over in the same place and that bruise would never go away. He never watched where he was running and he was constantly banging into things. I'm sure people must have thought I was abusing him.

I remember one day when I took him to work with me. He ran up the stairs ahead of me and was running so fast I couldn't catch him. I could see the giant post in the middle of the hall but I could only hope and pray he wouldn't go that way. Of course he did. Not only did he go that way but also he went running as fast as he could right into it. All the while he was looking back at me and I am looking ahead at the pole, trying to yell loud enough to scare him into stopping but that didn't happen. BANG, right into the pole and yet another huge black and blue on the top of the head. And there it was for an entire year, one bruise after another.

He was just a very active child and there was not one thing I could do about it even if I'd wanted to. Most of these injuries occurred before the age of two. I couldn't leave him for a second; he was just way too crazy. It seemed as though he didn't sleep at all either but despite this, he was still on the go, non-stop.

Once I found him on top of my refrigerator. I have no idea how he climbed that far up the counter and managed to get all the way on top of the fridge but he did it. He was as proud as a peacock up there. I couldn't even go into the bathroom without bringing him along.

One day he somehow managed to fall and bang his head on the toilet bowl while I was trying to pee as fast as I could. As I was holding his hand, he squirmed really hard and let go falling down between the toilet and the sink resulting in yet another huge black and blue bruise on his head. My mother-in-law told me that I should be watching him more closely. I know she didn't believe me when I told her that it had happened while I was trying to pee and hold his hand at the same time.

In his first year of life, before he walked, I was the one with the perpetual black and blue marks. His head seemed to be exceptionally hard and a little bit on the large size. My husband used to say that it was because he had a really big brain and that it was a good thing. The downside was that this head of his always managed to come down and slam me right in the face. It didn't matter what he was doing, he always led with his head and for some reason my face was the landing strip. I had a black eye off and on for an entire year. I hated going into my weekly staff meetings and having people ask me what happened week after week. I really do think they thought I had an abusive husband at home.

The year I had a chronic black eye, my husband and I went out for drinks on the fourth of July. We were standing at the bar waiting to order and the bartender kept ignoring us. I couldn't figure out why he wouldn't take our order, then it dawned on me—I had a huge shiner and he must have thought my husband had punched me out one night in a drunken stupor. We laughed about it later but it really wasn't so funny when it was actually happening. The embarrassing appearance aside, it really did hurt to be hit in the face so many times.

After my year of the black and blue ended, his began. When he was a little over two, he seemed to get a bit more coordinated and didn't fall as much but he was still climbing a lot and liked to swing from things. Three times he pulled his elbow out while swinging from the stair railings. It's referred to as "nursemaid's elbow" and I quickly learned how to put it back into place again. I never realized how many things I would have to learn as a mom, especially having a child like mine who seemed to have a great affinity for getting himself into mischief.

When he was about four and a half, he was jumping on the diving board in our backyard pool. Even back then he was a strong swimmer. During a family cookout, he was trying to show off how well he could jump off the board. All of a sudden, he started jumping up and down more frantically than usual. At first I thought he was just goofing around because that's the kind of kid he's always been, then I realized something else was going on. I could tell by the expression on his face that something bad had happened and right before he jumped into the water, he screamed bloody blue murder. He swam to the edge as fast as he could and was still screaming when he got out of the pool.

He ran over to me and told me that a bee had flown up his bathing suit. I couldn't believe my ears. He was telling the truth and sure enough, a bee had been under the diving board and had actually flown up into his shorts and stung him right on the tip of his penis. I was sick when I saw the red mark and even worse was the huge amount of swelling. I brought him inside and he took off his shorts, revealing testicles as large and red as two tomatoes. I felt helpless. One of the grandmothers at the cookout told us to put onions on it. This made him freak out even more. He was yelling and screaming saying, "You are NOT putting onions on my pee pee mom, that is disgusting." I had to call his doctor and when I explained the situation, they said that eventually the swelling would go down.

A few years after the traumatic bee sting incident, we were on a family vacation and he had yet another freak injury to his private parts. Just when I thought I couldn't be any more surprised by anything that happened to this kid, he somehow spilled bug spray down his pants. Trust me, I know how strange that seems but amazingly, he really did. We were in Maine, on our way to a drive-in Movie Theater when he said he had to pee really badly. I immediately pulled over to the side of the road.

One of the great things about having a boy is that they can pee anywhere. He opened the door and started to go about his business. As he was starting to pee, he accidentally knocked over a bottle of bug spray. It seems that the top had been loose and when it fell over, it came off. It started to spill out and with his bad luck, wouldn't you know? It spilled right onto his penis.

His screams got louder as it burned deeper and deeper through his skin. I jumped out of the car to see what was the matter and he was yelling that the bug spray spilled on his pee pee. How on earth could a bottle of bug spray open up and happen to just spill out right at that moment and land exactly in that spot? Well, now we know.

We had to find a bathroom immediately to wash him up. After we got everything cleaned up, he ended up having a massive stomach ache probably from all of the stress of the burning penis episode. He wound up on the toilet in a restaurant bathroom for half an hour. Needless to say we missed the movie at the drive-in but more importantly, my son was alright in the end. Since this story has gone from bruises to penises, I may as well mention a few other anecdotes about this particular subject. Fortunately my son has had no other injuries to that area of his body but he has had a few interesting things to say on the subject.

During a routine trip to the pediatrician for an annual physical the doctor began to examine my son from top to bottom. I had no idea what to expect when the doctor asked him to pull down his Buzz Lightyear underwear and much to my relief, he did as he was told and cooperated. The doctor was finishing up my son's examination and gave his testicles a quick squeeze. While I am sure this shocked my son very much, he didn't miss a beat in his response. He looked right up into the doctor's eyes and said, "Hey Doc, be careful with the family jewels, that's my livelihood you know!" I was stunned speechless and just stood there like any completely mortified mother would.

I knew right away where that comment had come from. We had been on a ski trip and ever the comedian, while he was in a bathroom with all of the older boys and his uncles, he decided to tuck his boy parts between his thighs and yell to all the other guys, "Hey look at me I'm a girl, I'm a girl!" They all cracked up and thought he was hilarious. However, one of his uncles was outraged and told him (very inappropriately I might add), "Do not mess with the family jewels, that's your livelihood!"

Yes, I know one might expect a comment like that coming from one of the older boys but his Uncle? I guess his words must have just slipped out from the shock of it all. It had been quite a few years since the Uncle in question has had little kids and I'm sure that was one of the last things he ever expected to see my son do.

Little did he know that his not so thoughtfully chosen words would come back to haunt me in the doctor's office. It did however, make for a lot of good laughs during our next family ski trip. Everybody thought it was the best story ever. Don't they always when they aren't the ones who have to suffer at the mercy of a quick-witted little comedian like mine?

Despite all of it, I do feel truly blessed to be his mom. It certainly makes for a very fun-filled and colorful life. Specifically the colors black and blue...and sometimes red.

Clammed Up

I HAD A FRIEND (WHO FOR OBVIOUS REASONS SHALL REMAIN NAMELESS) call me as she was on her way to the gynecologists' office for a "not so fresh" feeling. She'd been whining about a nasty yeast infection and we started cracking some ill-humored jokes about cheating husbands.

Our twisted minds are always conjuring up these scenarios about what husbands do, or more to the point, *who* they do when they are traveling out of town for business. She complained, "This is just my shit luck. We never have sex anymore and the one damn time I finally give it up, I get a raging yeast infection."

Although, I wouldn't necessarily disagree with her theory about shit luck, I had to remind her that she *had* just finished a dose of antibiotics. I said, "It's a natural reaction, when we lose not only our bad bacteria, but the good ones as well. Pair that with a lack of yogurt and there you have it! The perfect recipe for brewing bread, which is otherwise known as the grossly irritating condition: YEAST."

With everything else my busy friend had going on in her life, I'm not at all surprised that she didn't consider the potential side effects of antibiotics. I wasn't going to mention the reason for the antibiotics but what the hell? She *is* nameless after all. She had been taking antibiotics for a gigantic boil that had planted itself on her left ass cheek. The day she blurted out this information to me might have been the day we officially bonded. You gotta really trust somebody if you can tell them about a boil on your ass. It doesn't get much more personal than that.

As she was walking into the doctor's office, we ended the call, right after I wished her good luck. A couple of hours went by after our call and I still hadn't heard from her. When she finally called me back, she was out of her mind.

For all women, the mortification of a gynecological exam just goes without saying. It's certainly no picnic to be sprawled out half naked with only a paper gown over your mid-section. Add to that the icy cold speculum, the hard metal stirrups, all the pressing and pushing, it's an uncomfortable time AT BEST. Of course, that's not the worst of it, because to top it all off, there's an extremely bright, shining, light illuminating it all.

As if all of that wasn't bad enough, my friend had a nurse and a student in there together. "I couldn't believe it" she said to me, "Of all days, I have to be there it's the day when they are training the new girl! So now, it's not just a nurse and a doctor to worry about, but a third pair of curious eyes on me as well." She went on to tell me that as soon as the nurse took a look, she uttered alarmingly, "I can't believe this! Oh how terrible! I've never seen anything this bad! You are so swollen and red, you poor thing!"

For the life of me, I couldn't figure out how a nurse working day in and day out in the Gyn office had never seen anything that bad. Then again, I wasn't the one doing the examination.

Before I had a chance to analyze this point any further, my friend explained that just when she thought it couldn't get any worse, the nurse came out with, "Have you ever had herpes before dear?" Just hearing the word "Herpes" was enough to send my friend into a total frenzy. Everything around her was spinning and any other words spoken were merely a mumbled mixture of incoherent sounds. I was surprised that she didn't just drop dead right then and there on the table with her feet frozen in those awful stirrups for all eternity.

This is a woman who bleaches her toilets three times a day and has enough antibacterial hand soap to open up her own "Bath and Body Works" Store. "Herpes" was the last thing she'd ever expected to hear come out of that nurse's mouth, so now her mind was racing full speed ahead. "That son of a bitch! What a bastard! I just knew it! He must be cheating on me! Why else would she be asking me if I'd ever had herpes before?"

As she recounted her story in painful detail, I couldn't get over the irony. There we were, constantly entertaining outrageous "what if's" about cheating husbands and random diseases when, out of the clear blue, there it was in real life. With some nurse throwing it out there like it's no big deal. "Oh surely you've had a breakout before haven't you dear?" It was like she was talking about the common cold or some kind of flu.

Not that the initial shock ever really wore off, but once my friend was calm enough to respond; she was finally able to assure the nurse that, no, she had never had the disease in her life. She suggested to the nurse that maybe she should first have checked her records, which were lying there open right on the counter, before asking that kind of question.

I told my friend I was impressed that she'd actually spoken up to the nurse because usually, my friend is nothing more than a doormat, who lets everybody walk all over her. I still think a better option might have been for her to have plucked her foot out of the evil metal contraption and given that nurse a good, hard kick—right in her smug face.

When the doctor finally took a look for herself, much to my nameless friend's relief, she diagnosed her as having "The most severe yeast infection I have ever seen". Although the diagnosis wasn't pretty, it was certainly a hell of a lot better than the alternative the nurse had offered up.

I felt so badly for her when she told me that story. It wasn't really funny but by the end of the conversation, we were both laughing at how odd the whole situation had been. And just when I thought it couldn't get any *more* ridiculous, she told me that when she complained to her husband about the terrible things that had happened at the Gyn office, all he could say was, "I hope you're not cheating on *me*! You don't really have Herpes, do you?" As you can imagine, his question didn't go over well with my friend. Ah yes, there's nothing quite like the support of a caring and sympathetic husband to take the edge off of a rotten day.

Another friend shared a similar story with me. It wasn't quite as horrific, but still awful nevertheless. She too shall remain nameless, and also made an appointment at the Gyn for a yeast infection. Although she wasn't probed by a patronizing nurse about venereal diseases, she was insulted enough to file a complaint. She told me that before the doctor examined her, she was asked the usual series of questions. All very personal questions mind you, but very standard.

Despite her discomfort, she answered everything quickly and willingly. She would do anything to get rid of that itch! Just when she thought she was finished, she was hit with the most appalling question of all. The nurse glanced up at her with a look of deep concern and said, "Now you do always clean up after sex, don't you?" I don't think my friend could have been any more caught off guard than if they'd asked her what positions she liked best. What a completely ignorant thing to ask! What the hell was wrong with that nurse?

My friend was stunned speechless as she sat there, staring back at the nurse in shock. She was so insulted at the mere suggestion that her infection was caused by uncleanliness. She glared at the nurse with a blatant look of disgust, as she gave it right back to her saying, "I hardly think that my yeast infection is a result of not cleaning up after sex." This was so unbelievable and what was worse, the nurse persisted on the subject and didn't shut up until she had given her a full blown lecture on how "Sex is a very messy business and we must be diligent about cleaning up afterward."

At the end of the appointment, my friend filed a complaint with the Gyn office because she felt that the nurse was so out of line. She was angry and offended that something like that could even be up for discussion. She said, "I really wanted to storm out of there, and I wish I had more guts. I would have told that bitch right where to go but instead, I sat there like a fool waiting for the doctor." "I would've been out of there in a heartbeat." I said. Then she reminded me how good her doctor is and how long she had waited to get in to see her. It wouldn't be worth it to leave anyway. After all, if she'd left, what could she have done about the more pressing matter at hand? THE ITCH. She got a prescription, filed her complaint and sped out of there before she killed somebody.

My own Gyn story is not as agonizing or disturbing but embarrassing nonetheless. Years ago, before I was married, I ran into my Gyn doctor at a grocery store. He was in line right behind me. I recognized him first and my mind immediately started conjuring up escape plots before he saw me. But of course, nothing ever comes easy to me. There was a little old lady with a walker in front of me, preventing any possibility of fleeing the scene. There was nowhere to run and no place to hide. I cringed and forced a smile, as I said, "Oh hi Dr. X." I felt my face catch fire and turn bright red as he began making small talk.

All I could think about at that moment was how he had seen me naked and helpless on his exam table, while there he was talking to me about frozen yogurt. It was seriously freaking me out. I know, I know, they see it all the time and it's just another (you know what) to them but still, I couldn't focus on a single thing he was saying. I was too busy picturing him with the Pap smear slide in one hand and the big silver crank thing in the other.

Suddenly he blurted out, "You're not married, are you?" It was all I could do to keep myself from throwing up all over a box of Cheerios. How dare he hit on me right here in the middle of the supermarket? Especially after seeing me inside and out, top to bottom? I thought, "This can't actually be happening, can it?" I was trying to pull myself together when he said, "I didn't see a ring on your left finger, but I figured I'd enquire because I have a younger brother who's single and I think you would be perfect for him."

I wanted to ask him, "Okay, and on what grounds am I perfect for your brother exactly?" All I could imagine was how he'd be sitting around with his brother talking about my last excursion with his cold, wet KY jelly. I was sweating profusely and searching for an explanation as to reasons I wouldn't be perfect for his single brother.

I have no idea why but I found myself apologizing to my doctor for having a serious boyfriend. My grocery cart was practically up on two wheels as I flew out of there, almost taking out a couple of baggers in the process. When I got home and looked in the mirror, my face was still redder than a Christmas stocking. Thankfully, by the time I had my annual exam, he had left the practice. That's when I decided to switch to a female gynecologist.

I'm sure every woman has her own horror stories about gynecologist appointments, which is just a sad fact of life. I know that *none* of us enjoy our annual visits, no matter how much our doctors try to be congenial. Even on the rare occasion when a compliment comes your way during an exam, that can be awkward too as well as hard to take.

I have a friend who was sprawled out on the table one day when her doctor told her she had done a fantastic job shaving. He happily proclaimed to her, "That's the best shaving job I have ever seen." I can't even imagine hearing that one.

Maybe Gynecologists shouldn't be allowed to talk at all. Perhaps the rule of thumb should be that they keep their mouths shut while our legs are open. They can surely say everything they need to say once our clothes are back on, when we can defend ourselves better.

If you think about it, there really isn't much that you *do* want to hear when you're on that table. After all, we all know the drill. Why do they always have to say, "Scoot down a little more, a little more, move your butt down, just a little bit more, there you go! Now legs down, feet here, relax now, just open up a little bit more and relax.

How can anybody relax in that position? Even if you do somehow manage to relax, one poke by the salad tongs and it's all over. While I would hate to be asked about Herpes or after sex clean up habits while lying there, I would equally hate to be told that I did a fantastic job shaving.

The more I think about it, the more I am convinced that if doctors are going to insist on talking during an exam, they should consider serving wine in the waiting room. Better yet, they should drink wine before the appointment too. That way, everyone is equally relaxed.

If the wine idea doesn't work, they should walk in with only a paper sheet around their midsection so we're all on equal footing. Then both the doctor, as well as the patient, can *truly* let it all hang out.

The Lynching of Mrs. Z.

THIRD GRADE STARTED OUT FOR MY SON as, what we had feared, would be his worst year in elementary school. The first week was absolutely rotten! Maybe I would have felt differently about it if there had been some type of warning. A red flag, a smoke signal, semaphore—anything. But I never saw it coming, which was probably a very good thing. It was the first time we'd ever experienced such a rollercoaster with a teacher.

The year had started out just like all other school years normally do, with the invitation to a class orientation over the summer. There were seven third grade classes that year and according to all of the kids at school, at least four out of the seven teachers were HORRIBLE.

All summer long my son Tommy prayed every night that he wasn't going to get one of the wretched teachers with a scary reputation. When it was time to check the class assignments, he breathed a huge sigh of relief when he saw he had gotten a new teacher named Mrs. Z. He pitied his friends who didn't have the same good fortune as he did. He had a smile from ear to ear.

The funny thing was we had never even heard of this Mrs. Z. Somehow that didn't matter to Tommy. He only cared that he hadn't been assigned to one of the four dreaded monsters. I, of course, wasn't as optimistic as my young son and decided to ask around to see what I could dig up. Most people had never heard the name, "Mrs. Z." before either. I couldn't seem to find out much of anything about her and I wasn't sure if that was a good thing or a bad thing. No matter what, it did seem a little strange.

Finally some information surfaced about the mysterious Mrs. Z. It turned out that one of my friend's sons had Mrs. Z. a few years earlier when she had been a fifth grade teacher. My friend said Mrs. Z. was great, so hearing that from her was both a major relief and wonderful news. I could hardly wait to tell my son that he really *did* luck out and in fact, had been assigned to one of the few "really nice" third grade teachers.

The night of third grade orientation went smoothly. I was surprised to see that Mrs. Z. was so young. She didn't even look old enough to drink legally. And yet, mathematically that made no sense because she had admitted to being in her sixth year of teaching. She said she was a newlywed and had a brand new last name, which explained why I hadn't been able to uncover much about her. With a brand new name and teaching a new grade, it was as though she was incognito.

Mrs. Z. stood there in front of us all while going through the usual orientation paperwork. She looked as sweet and fuzzy as a peach. She had an airy quality about her, a voice like an angel and kind eyes. Her hair was shiny blond and she was dressed adorably. She easily could have passed for Barbie's little sister, Skipper.

Well, one thing is certain, looks can be very deceiving. It didn't take either Tommy or me too long to figure out that Mrs. Z. was something completely the opposite of "sweeter than sweet". A more appropriate description might have been "stricter than strict".

I had a teacher like that when I was in the second grade. She was worse than the Wicked Witch of the West but at least she looked the part. Anybody who saw her coming could immediately tell she was an old witch. She was grotesque and frightening. She had oily skin, ratty red hair, and even had a bald spot on the top of her head to complete the perfect stereotype of a hag.

She scared the daylights out of me and I can remember living in terror every single dreaded day that school year. As a matter of fact, I still see her in church occasionally and it gives me goose bumps just to look at her. She's gotta be 100 years old by now and I can't believe that she hasn't been run down by some traumatized former student. It's a good thing she gets herself to church because that woman has a lot of repenting to do.

We hadn't even gotten through the first week of school with Mrs. Z. when Tommy came home with a "sad bird" in his backpack. We were warned about the "sad bird" at orientation, but we only half paid attention because we never figured Tommy would ever bring one home.

If a child missed an assignment, Mrs. Z. would send home a picture of a sad bird. It looked more like a deranged pelican than a sad bird to me, but she said it was her way of communicating with the parents of her students.

According to one of the other parents, they were called "mad birds" when she taught fifth grade but now for third grade, they had been changed to "sad birds". For a minute, I thought that when she had changed the name of the birds, it demonstrated sympathy for the third graders but I soon found out that it did not matter to Mrs. Z. whether her students were fifth graders or third graders, they would all be treated equally. We discovered that really wasn't such a good thing. It was becoming abundantly clear that although Mrs. Z. may have been spending her days in a third grade classroom, in her mind and actions she was still teaching fifth grade.

It was not a pleasant day at my house the day Tommy returned home with a "sad bird" in his backpack. He had never been in trouble in school for any reason and has always completed all of his assignments. I was as surprised as he was when he got this abrupt insult with less than a full week of school finished.

Despite the fact that all of his written assignments had been completed, he hadn't brought in his spelling words. For the past two years he had been asked to write his spelling words nightly but was never required to turn them in the following day. Based on past history, we assumed that he still didn't have to bring them in—Big mistake!

I signed my initials on Tommy's homework sheet stating that he *had* completed the assigned spelling words. I figured my signature was worth something to a teacher, but apparently it wasn't to Mrs. Z. It didn't seem to matter what I said or if I signed in blood. Unless she had those spelling words in her hand, she was not going to believe either my son or me. I envisioned her smiling as she happily filled out that ridiculous sad bird and sent it home with my poor, unsuspecting child. If she had any idea of the chaos she was inducing in my home that night, then she was even crueler than I figured her to be.

First, my son blamed me because I was the one who'd told

him that he didn't need to turn in his spelling words. Then he started blaming himself while crying and pounding his fists on the kitchen table. Then it was onto Mrs. Z., and what a god awful, horrible, mean teacher she was and how could she give him a sad bird in the first place?

Now he felt the fear of potential detention and ultimately, suspension and it wouldn't be long before he was a third grade flunkey heading to juvie. He was so upset he said he never wanted to return to school again. He found himself wishing for those four teachers with the notorious reputations because anything would be better than dealing with the wrath of Mrs. Z.

Being his mother, I did the only thing I could think of to do: I wrote a double sided note to his teacher explaining everything. I tried in vain to take the blame and did nothing short of begging her to remove that sad bird from his record. I explained how conscientious my child was and how serious he takes such things. I told her that he was worried sick that this would affect his report card and that he was practically having a nervous breakdown over it.

I was proud of the finished product when the note was done. I was certain she would return an apology note and retract the sad bird. I even envisioned her killing the damn bird and sending me home the dead body. No such luck.

I did get a letter back, although it wasn't at all what I expected. She simply said that she felt that the sad birds were important for communication purposes and that in the future Tommy should turn in "ALL of his assignments".

That was it—clearly there was no reasoning with this woman. Now I was ready for war! About a week went by and Tommy got his first project. He had to make a Compass Rose. Since both my husband and I were worried about the long lasting effects of that stupid sad bird, we decided that we couldn't possibly do enough to help this poor kid. We sat with him for hours and tediously worked on that compass rose. We stopped at nothing to make sure it was right. We even had his Papa helping. It was a family affair.

We not only did what the instructions said to do but we went way above and beyond. Yes, I do realize this sounds a bit fanatical but you just don't know my kid. Saying he is anal and even paranoid about his schoolwork would be an understatement. So there we were, almost the entire family, working on this 3rd Grade Project.

We painstakingly cut out all of the arrows. We went on the Internet and found a superb design idea and we pooled all of our creativity and constructed one truly amazing compass rose. Did I mention this was a THIRD GRADE project?

Tommy was thrilled and so excited to turn in his project. He couldn't wait to get his grade. It seemed like it took forever to get it back but I knew in my heart that he would get a 100%. How could he not? He had all of us working on it, right? I mean, you can't tell me that our entire family isn't smarter than a third grader?

The day arrived when the project finally came home with a grade. I remember that day as if it were yesterday. I was working and my husband was home to get our kids off the bus. He was the one who first laid eyes on the grade. It wasn't so much the grade that was the issue but the little comments written in orange at the bottom of the paper.

My husband looked it over and decided that the best course of action would be to hide the paper from me. He knew that if

I came home from work and saw the grade and worse yet, the comments, it wouldn't be pretty for him or anybody else in the family.

It wasn't long after I came home that I asked Tommy about the project. I knew it had to have been returned by now. He told me that he got it back that day and to go ask Daddy for it.

I immediately went to my husband with excited anticipation. I couldn't wait to see the A+. When I asked my husband where the paper was, he wouldn't tell me. I didn't understand why he was playing games with me. It had been a long day and I wanted the paper. He just kept saying, "Oh god, you are not going to be happy about this one!" Of course, this made me even more curious and now I was practically begging to see the paper. He reluctantly gave in and went in the drawer and took it out from its hiding spot.

She gave him a 90%. Not so bad really. Then I saw it. The comment my husband didn't want me to see. At the bottom of the paper, she wrote a note asking us to, "Please let Tommy do his own projects". My husband was right. I was *not* happy. Not happy at all. In that moment, I no longer liked Mrs. Z., not even a little bit.

The night for Parent/Teacher Conferences, both of Tommy's grandmothers wanted to go so that they could give Mrs. Z. a piece of their mind. Fortunately for Mrs. Z., it ended up being just my husband and me. I listened patiently to everything she had to say and just as I was about to tell her how I really felt, my husband stopped me. I was so blown away by what he said next, I didn't know what to say.

He looked at her, smiled and came out with, "Mrs. Z., I think you are the greatest teacher there ever was. Every teacher should be like you. If all kids had a teacher like you, they would all succeed in life. The stricter you are, the better, and if there's ever a lynch mob after you, I'll have your back."

I went into complete shock. I didn't actually have any idea what a lynch mob even was. I thought I was going to slap him right across the face. I did manage to kick him under the table a few times. How could he say those things to her after what she had done to my poor little baby? The worst part was, he never even discussed any of it with me beforehand.

I was speechless after he stabbed me in the back like that and didn't end up talking to him until later that night. I said, "Why did you say all of those nice things to that mean Mrs. Z.? And what the hell is a lynch mob anyway?" He told me that he knew our son would do well with a lot of structure and he liked her style. He said that he thought that Tommy needed a challenge and she was the perfect teacher to give it to him. He went on to tell me that a lynch mob would be a group of angry mothers trying to get her hanged. I was disturbed at that thought, but more disturbed that he was such a traitor.

In the end, I did understand where my husband was coming from, but my first instinct was to protect my child. The school year grew to a close, and as much as I hate to admit it, I could see that my husband had been 100% right. Mrs. Z., did in fact, turn out to be the best teacher my son has ever had.

She remained strict but very consistent, predictable and challenging. The proof was in the pudding and Tommy really thrived with Mrs. Z. and his last report card was nearly perfect. He managed to get 100's on all of his tests and quizzes and never once got a "sad bird" again.

To this day, he raves about how much he loved Mrs. Z. and

how much he loved third grade. I was completely wrong about her and I am thrilled to admit it.

One day in the final term of the school year, Tommy forgot to bring in his spelling words, but Mrs. Z. didn't give him a sad bird. He didn't even mention the incident to me, until the following day when he came across his spelling words. He said, "Oh Mom, these are the words that I forgot to bring in yesterday." I said, "What are you talking about? What do you mean you forgot to bring them in?" He said, "Don't worry mom, Mrs. Z. knows I'm trustworthy and when I told her they were done she believed me and she didn't even give me a sad bird." Wow, I was so shocked! Talk about coming full circle!

Throughout the school year, Tommy and Mrs. Z. had a formed a wonderful relationship, which I couldn't have imagined that first week of school. I never thought I would say this in a million years, but any kid who gets Mrs. Z. for a teacher will be a very lucky kid indeed.

During teacher appreciation day, my husband and I brought in sandwiches for all of the teachers. Tommy told me to be sure that Mrs. Z. got a huge Italian and I made certain I did exactly as he had asked. I told her that it was very important to Tommy that she get *that* particular sandwich and she seemed to really appreciate it.

That huge Italian sandwich looked a lot better than what I had to eat that day: Crow with a nice slice of humble pie. Under the circumstances though, seeing my son so happy and knowing he'd had such a great year at school, that crow was actually pretty delicious.

And I know for a fact that crow surely tasted a lot better than having to force down a "sad bird".

The Saving Cup

AFTER ALL THESE YEARS OF TAKING MY KIDS TO CHURCH you might think I would have learned by now that they are not going to behave there. I mean, if GOD can't get them to sit still, how could I possibly ever think that I am going to?

I continually try to figure out how an hour long Mass can feel like it takes ten hours to get through. No matter how many things I used to bring with me solely for their entertainment, inevitably they would become bored and start acting up.

Even when my eldest child was practically a teenager, I kept it up. I'll admit that I'm impressed with myself for sticking it out as long as I did. I've been dragging my son to church since he was a newborn baby and it's been anything but easy—just like him. I have no idea how it is that I haven't quit forcing him to go after over a decade of Mass mishaps. Maybe I enjoy the torture?

Before the age of two, my son had quite an impressive vocabulary. I might have mentioned that? Although most of the words he could say did make me proud, like "Chinese Silk Moth." Some of them would make me shudder, like "Fucka Bitch".

From birth it felt like he was absorbing everything all the time. Including all kinds of vocabulary words, both good and bad. Thanks to his older siblings, he knew many words I'd rather he didn't know.

One Sunday morning during Mass, the priest was preaching a homily where he was saying the words, "Jesus Christ" repeatedly. After about the fifth time he said it, my son blurted out, "Jesus Christ? Mom, did he just say Jesus Christ? That is a bad word." It seemed as though everybody in the entire church heard my son and they were all staring at us trying to suppress their laughter. It was surely not one of our better church moments. I was stoic on the outside, but suffering on the inside. Then again, I think that was probably the point of the homily that day. It was all about what Jesus did for all of the suffering of mankind.

Taking the homily to heart, I figured I should be able to withstand a bit of suffering myself. Maybe the homily that day was God's way of driving the point home directly to me. Then somewhere between the offertory and the "Our Father" prayer, my son decided to yank my blouse down and show off my bra while yelling, "Boobies" as loud as he possibly could. That should have been the straw that broke the camel's back, yet we voyaged on.

On another occasion, he reached his arm over the pew and grabbed a woman's hair. It was bad enough to see him put the grab on her but when I realized that she was wearing a wig, I gasped in fear. I saw the hair shift in a way that wasn't normal and I got queasy, as if I knew what was coming next. Thankfully God was on my side that morning and he let go before the entire thing came flying off. Phew...what a disaster that could have been!

Another time during a night mass, I was desperate to keep

him quiet so I took my wedding rings off and let him play with them. Despite the fact that it was against my better judgment I did it anyway. Within minutes all that was heard was the clink, clink, clink, sound of my rings hitting the wood floor as they rolled noisily. People six and even seven pews up were bending down searching under their seats for my wedding rings.

I thought I was gonna lose it when my husband shot me a glare that screamed, "How could you let him play with those?" It was terrible to constantly put ourselves at this child's mercy but again, isn't God merciful?

Fortunately, as he's gotten older, we don't have as much trouble getting him to behave in church. I think by this stage of the game I have perfected the threatening look and he knows that when I give it to him, I mean business.

Much to my relief, I haven't had to employ "the look" on very many occasions in recent years. A few years ago, we had a situation where I had to use "the look" and back then, I wasn't sure if it was gonna work. It was a difficult and dreadful situation, and one that called for immediate praying for my son to adhere to my warning.

During a rehearsal for Communion, one of the kids in our congregation got in the line for the wine, but had no intention of drinking from the cup. When he realized what he had done, he quickly bypassed the woman holding the cup and snuck back to his seat. It was comical to watch the first time, but when we saw him make the same mistake twice, all of the parents got a kick out of the look on his face when he realized he had done it again.

There were a few giggles in the crowd of parents but there was a very loud sound heard above the giggles, which was the unmistakable sound of the accidental passing of gas. It was probably heard throughout the church and was difficult to ignore. Although, as is usually the case with this type of situation, most people did their best to pretend that nothing had happened. After all, that is the decent thing to do. No one there would ever want it to happen to us and we know that the first rule of good karma is to politely ignore such an offense.

I knew immediately by the look on my son's face that, just like the rest of us, he knew what he heard. My son was eight years old at that time and boys that age are not only experts on all things that are gross or inappropriate, they also take great pride in such things.

I had no idea what he was about to do but no matter what it was, I figured it wouldn't be good. I knew one thing for sure, he didn't know where it came from and I wasn't about to turn around to find out. Sure, I was curious too, but I knew if I turned around or acknowledged it in any way, shape or form it would only escalate matters.

Unfortunately, the guilty party, a mom, was all too proper and a lady through and through. She did the socially appropriate thing and excused herself—out loud. Although I give her credit for her willingness to ask to be excused publicly, I was terrified, because by this admission, my son now knew for certain who the culprit was.

I was positive he was surely going to make a big deal out of the awkwardness of the moment thereby drawing all the more attention to this already uncomfortable situation. He was about to open his mouth when I employed "the look".

"The look" I gave him that morning was even more threatening than my usual look. It was the look that said in no uncertain terms, "If you dare open your mouth, I may beat you right here on the spot in front of all of your friends, their parents, the priest and God himself." He got the message and although he was cracking up with his hands over his face, he did manage to contain his laughter. I had a hard enough time keeping my own laughter at bay because as soon as I turned around and saw Chrissy a couple of rows back, she too, looked like she was about to faint.

We exchanged a thankful glance as if to say, "Oh man, that so could have been you or me...thank god for small miracles." Of course it was Chrissy's son who had gone to the saving cup twice and in a way had actually caused the whole situation to happen.

It certainly did make for some hilarious bedtime material for my kid. He made up songs, spoofs and even created his own cartoon about it. I was simply grateful that he was old enough to decipher "the look" and to actually fear it.

Lest you think my son is the only recipient of "the look", do not despair! I have utilized it for other family members as well. Many Christmas Eve's ago, I thought about giving my own mother "the look".

My husband and I always invite my parents to our Catholic Parish to celebrate Christmas Mass with us, even though they aren't Catholic. Just as the Communion was about to be offered, I looked over and saw my mother break out a Ziploc bag filled with tiny broken up pieces of bread. Now I've heard of BYOB parties but thought, "C'mon mom! Really?"

I was so surprised, but hey who am I to judge her, right? I myself was not even fully Catholic at the time, although for over a year I had been in the process of converting. Since I couldn't receive Communion, I suppose maybe Mom's bag of bread might have been better than nothing, but still, who was going to bless this bread? It was a mystery to me and I was surprised to say the least. Except I wasn't as surprised as when moments later, I found out that my husband and I were expected to bring the bread and wine to the altar during this very same Mass.

I guess it's some unwritten Catholic rule that if nobody else gets up to carry the bread and wine to the altar, then the people sitting in the seat directly behind the table that holds it, should kindly oblige. Well, just my luck, we happened to be seated in the hot spot.

I saw a man come down the aisle with a bag of money, and he nudged my husband and then my husband nudged me. Because it was Christmas Eve, the church was spilling over with people that night. He nudged me again and I nudged him back harder as I looked at him like he was out of his mind. My first reaction was to shake my head motioning no. As I said, I was not a Catholic yet so how would I ever know what to do with the Holy Communion?

All eyes were on me as I continued to shake my head desperately trying to convey, "Oh no, no thank you honey, I'll pass on this one." My husband practically pushed me off the chair as it became increasingly obvious that denial was not an option. The events remain a bit foggy in my mind, and I think I may have still been holding my mother's little pieces of bread in my hand at the time. I was no more sure of what to do when she handed me the Ziploc bag of her own bread as I was when my husband was pointing at the silver bowl full of the Holy Eucharist on the table.

Eventually, I realized that I wasn't going to get away with just sitting there on the pew shaking my head no, so I had to get up and follow my husband. He has been a Catholic his entire life so I figured he damn well better have known what he was doing by that point. He took the body and I picked up the blood and we walked toward the altar together in front of what felt like a million watchful eyes.

I had gone to that church for ten years and never before had been asked to do what we were doing at that very moment. As a matter of fact, most of the time I would see people just get up and do it without being asked. I never knew if it was planned ahead or if people took it upon themselves to participate. I got quite the Catholic education that night when I learned the hard way about the unwritten rule of the people who sit behind the table of the Holy Communion.

I was a nervous wreck because I didn't know what the heck I was supposed to do when I got up to the priest at the altar. Like so many other things in my life, I had to wing it. I was shaking from head to toe when I walked up that aisle. In the end, it all seemed to work out well because somehow I managed to get the wine up there and by the grace of God, I didn't spill a drop.

I was in shock for the rest of the Mass and I think I ended up stuffing that little piece of bread from my mom's bag into my coat pocket. As disgusting as it might sound, that little piece of bread is probably still there because I know I never ate it.

The entire experience was daunting for me but all in all, I believe that it was meant to be that night above all other nights. I always felt sad when my son went up for Communion but my husband and I couldn't, so it really was a gift to be included in that way. BYOB or not, we survived the experience and it was a beautiful Mass.

I think the next time we invite my parents to attend Christmas

Eve Mass with us, I'll ask my mom if she could possibly bring a flask filled with wine along with her little bag of bread. I won't have any objections to that.

Now that I have become a Catholic, I can say with great certainty that when it's time for me to receive The Holy Communion, I solemnly promise that no one will ever see me bypassing that saving cup. I assure you, nobody needs it quite as much as I do.

French Martini Mayhem

IT'S FUNNY HOW ALL SORTS OF THINGS CAN GET TIED TO
PARTICULAR EVENTS, which inevitably make it impossible to
separate them ever again. Take French Martinis; for me, they
will be forever linked to my friend Sue. More specifically, French
Martinis are forever linked to my friend Sue at her husband's
Christmas Party.

The incident occurred several years ago, although it is as
clear in my mind now as if it had happened yesterday. Sue had
called to fill me in on the details of her husband's company
Christmas party the night before. And, according to her, things
didn't go so well at the party.

After I hung up the phone with Sue, I wondered if her husband still had his job. The night probably wouldn't have taken
such a turn for the worse if only they had served Beringer White
Zinfandel at the party. Sue loves White Zinfandel, especially
Beringer! It's her absolute favorite and she was more than a
little disappointed to find out that even though the company
party had an open bar, there wasn't a drop of White Zin in the

place, never mind her preferred brand: Beringer.

Even though Sue couldn't remember the name of the place where the party was held, it would be a safe bet to assume that it was too classy to serve cheap wine. I know this because several months before the dreaded Christmas party, Sue and I went with our husbands to the opening of an upscale restaurant located in downtown Boston, probably in the same vicinity. We'd never been there before, and there was about a half hour wait, so we decided to sit at the bar. I ordered a glass of Merlot, and she ordered her usual, Beringer White Zinfandel. Although we'd ordered, and been served, these same drinks more times over the years than I would care to admit, this time was different.

The bartender glared at us with an obvious look of disgust. He gave us both the once over by looking us up and down and finally fixed his gaze on Sue. I think he was trying to force a sympathetic smile but his face contorted into more of a grimace as he said in slow motion, "We do not serve White Zinfandel here. You may want to consider trying our house Riesling instead. Our house Riesling is a more sophisticated wine and I think your palate will find it quite pleasing."

In other words, "Why don't you two classless bitches go back to the street where you came from and drink your cheap shit booze out of a paper bag?" Our husbands said nothing, as we both looked at each other totally appalled that this jerk was so blatantly condescending.

Fast forward to the Company Christmas Party, which as I said, must have been at a very classy place in Boston. Once again, Sue found herself being denied her beverage of choice. Unfortunately for my dear friend, her memory is not as good as mine. If only she had called me from the bar, I would have reminded her that according to snooty bartenders, *sophisticated* women don't drink Zinfandel. They drink Riesling.

Sadly, Sue took matters into her own hands and decided to order a French Martini. Again, calamity could have been avoided if only she had called me. I would have told her that drinking anything containing Vodka at her husband's holiday party could only signal imminent disaster.

The first three went down fast and easy. The colors in the room sparkled more vibrantly, the dance floor became more electric and the party was now nothing short of a rocking blast. Those French Martinis were so divine that she convinced one of the other wives to start drinking them with her. Three turned into four and four into five. This was the best company party ever!

Now, here is the difference between drinking White Zinfandel and drinking French Martinis: With the wine, you can actually feel the buzz start creeping up on you. You may start slurring your words and even staggering a bit after a few glasses, but somehow you know that you have to slow it down.

This is *not* the case with French Martinis. It appears that in less than a fragment of a second, you can go from being completely relaxed to completely out of your ever-loving mind.

Forget the buzz, there is no buzz. This is not a drink for amateurs, and not something you drink four or five of, *especially* not at your husband's company Christmas Party. Sue learned this lesson the hard way.

She watched with foggy eyes, as her drinking buddy Christine grabbed one of her husband's co-workers and headed out to the dance floor. Christine's husband, who was a very close friend of Sue's husband, watched as his wife threw herself all over a man on the dance floor. She could barely stand up, let alone dance.

As drunk as Sue was, she knew she was no better off than Christine. Yet somehow, she managed not to drag some poor, unsuspecting, junior executive out onto the dance floor. She would've *liked* to peel her friend off the man on the dance floor, but at that point, she had her own problems. She pleaded in vain to get her own husband to take her home before the something bad that she knew was about to happen...happened.

There was no such luck for Sue. Her husband was either ignoring her or (more likely) didn't give a shit. Somehow he saw the more important mission of the moment as prying his friend's wife Christine off of the man she was grinding up against on the dance floor. He must have felt it his honorable duty to protect his friend from any further humiliation.

Although it may have been rather righteous of him to worry about his co-worker and his drunken wife, where the hell was the loyalty here? What about his *own* wife who was desperately sinking further into Martini Mayhem? I'm sure he was proud of himself when he successfully got Christine off the dance floor and returned her safely to her husband, Bill. But I'm pretty sure he wasn't proud when he turned around to see his own wife slumped over on the bar.

Sue woke up the next morning with a pounding headache and a huge wad of gum stuck in her hair. She didn't remember the ride home but did notice what looked an awful lot like puke all over the outside doors of the family minivan. She had a huge visible welt on her forehead, which must have been where her head hit the bar, as well as a mysterious and gigantic lump on the back of her head. Much to Sue's dismay and her husband's disgrace, he literally had to carry her out (and off) of the bar.

Isn't it ironic that if she had only been permitted to drink her cheap wine, she would've been able to maintain the image of a sophisticated, classy, executive's wife? And yet, she was forced to drink a more *sophisticated* cocktail only to find herself slumped over the bar and passed out cold. Which was definitely not so classy—not at all.

I guess maybe husband and wife both learned a lesson that night. For the husband: When your wife tells you she needs to leave, "right now" you damn well better give a shit and do what she says. You fail to comply with that command at your own peril. For the wife: Invest in a good flask and never leave home without your own drink of choice. Especially if it's Beringer White Zinfandel.

Waiter, there's a fly in my soup!

DIVORCE REALLY SUCKS. No doubt about it. No matter who you are, whether you're the person who left, or the one left behind, there's nothing pretty about divorce. Unless you're actually the divorce lawyer and are cashing in on that new condo in Boca. With such high divorce rates and even higher wedding bills, it's amazing anyone gets married anymore.

Even though the majority of newlyweds can quote that the current divorce rate in America is hovering around 51% for first time marriages, and around 72% for subsequent marriages, we all know it's hard to face facts and statistics when you fall in love.

How exciting it is to envision the happiest day of your life? It feels like the whole world is at your fingertips, with all of your hopes and dreams stretched out in front of you. You picture the American Dream in all of its splendor. You can see it all before you: the big beautiful house, the handsome husband, the kids and the dog—even the brightly blooming flowers in the front garden.

Then reality kicks in.

We realize that even if we do manage to get any of these things on the list, the "real life" version is hardly ever even close to the dream. Ignorance is bliss, so you take the plunge.

A few years later, that big beautiful house has a big ugly mortgage draining you month after miserable month. The handsome husband now has a beer gut and spends most nights glued to the TV watching football. The kids never stop fighting, the dog is pissing all over the rug and the flowers in the front garden are so thirsty they are wilting before your eyes. It's easy for people to crumble under the weight of these pressures and it happens to the best of couples. It happened to my friend Trish.

It's hard enough to pick up the pieces and move on after having seen your marriage ripped to shreds, but one of the worst things about divorce, is that after you've been torn asunder, it's time to start dating again.

Dating in general is tough. But dating after divorce? It can be a bloodbath. Even *if* you manage to get past your trust issues, your fears and cynicism–it can still be really depressing.

Getting back into the dating scene after a breakup is always hard but it's especially brutal when you're on the wrong side of 30 and specifically after you've had a couple of kids. It's an entirely different story when you have to put yourself back out there on the market after your body has been tortured and stretched to accommodate a living growing human being inside.

If the body image issues aren't bad enough, then there's the fact that most of your friends are still married, so how do you meet somebody? Particularly, when you spend most of your time at the playground or running around with a toddler under your toes.

Even if you're fortunate enough to find a non-commitment phobic, non-gay and non-married guy, he surely won't be good looking. It's hard enough to find a date never mind finding a dependable babysitter, arranging a time to go out and then having to pay for the childcare on top of it all.

The whole idea is overwhelming and I don't know how Trish could deal with it day in and day out. I still can't believe that her husband even left her. He is a complete idiot. That's the only logical explanation possible. He, like so many other jerks out there just woke up one day and decided it was too much work and not enough fun being a responsible and mature adult.

He figured it was time to get out and try to recapture whatever he thought was left of his youth. He wanted to run for the hills, leave it all behind—his wife, kids, and mortgage—and never look back. "It's just not my thing." He explained to Trish when he left.

While Trish did receive a generous settlement and will get by fine, there is no amount of compensation in this world that could ever fill the hole he drilled through her heart.

One night the troops rallied to take her out for dinner. There were six of us: Trish, Chrissy, Janie, Mo, Kelly and me. We were doing everything in our power to bring Trish out of her post-divorce depression. We arrived at our agreed upon destination, a restaurant we figured would be just the thing to lighten Trish's heavy heart.

Our table wasn't ready yet so we sat at the bar. The bar was an alluring place to sit and suddenly, we *all* felt a little bit single. I'd met most of these women through my kid's Catholic preschool. I used to think all Catholic mommies were reserved and responsible just like they appeared to be at all the "mommy teas" held at school. I soon uncovered their little farce.

When *these* mommies got out, they were the worst kind of trouble—or the best kind. It all depends on your perspective.

From my perspective, the worst kind of trouble was the best kind of fun.

We hadn't even gotten the appetizers yet when Janie starting telling us about her new vibrator. As many times as we've heard Janie's bold confessions, she still managed to catch some of us off guard. Before anyone had a chance to comment on the sex toy of the month, Kelly blurted out that she and her husband Greg watched porn together all of the time. Janie chimed in that she too enjoyed watching adult flicks and had never been more supportive of her husband going on business trips since she purchased her new "purple passion".

A half hour passed at the bar and Chrissy was bullshit that the waitress still hadn't brought our appetizers yet. We all knew that if she didn't eat soon, things were gonna get ugly.

I called the waitress over to inquire about our food, just as Mo was showing off her new diamond necklace. It was a gorgeous silver chain with an "M" made of diamonds dangling from it. I told her immediately that I was sorry if I offended her, but it looked more like two penises hanging together off the chain than the letter "M". Everyone else agreed. A little while later, she admitted that when her husband gave her the new necklace, he also gave her some cash and told her to go out and buy some sex toys. She was convinced he was kidding.

"Well, no wonder he gave you the penis necklace! The guy is trying to tell you something and he was dead serious when he asked you to go buy sex toys." I said. With burning cheeks Mo said, "I have never even *seen* a sex toy, let alone used one! I wouldn't have the faintest idea where to buy one or even WHAT to buy for that matter." She hesitated, and then added, "Plus, I wouldn't do it even if he begged me to. And besides, he was kidding, don't you think?" she asked naively.

We had to tell her one hundred and one times that he wasn't kidding but she still didn't believe us. Chrissy was relieved when the appetizers finally arrived and I couldn't help but roll my eyes when Mo ordered another club soda with a lime. I had to bite my tongue as I thought about telling her to loosen up and have a damn drink for once. I could only imagine that it had to be painful for her to be that much of a straight edge all the time.

This was all a great distraction for Trish who was at least getting some good comic relief. Unfortunately, despite all of the fun we'd been having and the light mood we'd created, our rug was about to be ripped right out from under us.

Chrissy got up to go to the bathroom and Janie started dialing a number on her cell phone. We still didn't have our table yet but Janie said it would be worth the wait because we were gonna sit by the fireplace. We didn't know who she was calling but soon enough we heard her inviting whomever it was to come on over and join us for some drinks.

Janie was already a couple of vodkas deep and sounded all too flirtatious on the phone. I found myself getting a little concerned and tried to be as nonchalant as possible when I asked, "Janie, do I even wanna know who you just invited to share drinks with us?" In her typical, brazen Janie way, she responded with an evil little cackle and said, "Oh stop being such a worry wart for God's sakes! It's just my husband's best friend and a couple of his buddies." She gushed about this single guy named Ed. She loved him to pieces and said that he was the nicest guy you'd ever want to meet. She thought he would be just *perfect* for Trish.

We were appalled. We all knew it was way too soon for Trish to think about dating. The ink wasn't even dry on her divorce papers yet. I briefly entertained the idea as to whether or not I should ask why Janie's husband's best friend and his buddies were invited, while he was conveniently left out of the loop, but I thought better of it and decided to keep my mouth shut.

When Chrissy came out of the bathroom she asked what all the commotion was about. Janie was trying to convince us that it would be fine and that Ed was really nice. Finally Trish said to her, "Janie, everybody knows when people describe a guy as 'nice', it's obviously because he's not attractive". Janie defended him with every breath. She kept saying how she knew Trish was gonna love him and he was such a great catch she couldn't understand how he could still be single.

None of us wanted to hang out with a group of guys that night. It defeated the entire purpose of a girl's night out and Trish had no intention of embarking on some awkward first blind date. Before we got out our final protests there they were—the three stooges. And they were heading straight for us. The first guy was a giraffe and I thought he was going to bang into the light fixture hanging from the ceiling. The second guy was hiding under a baseball cap. The third guy? Well, he had to be Ed. Janie was right. He wasn't ugly. He was "just crawled out from under a rock" ugly.

He reminded me of that Sesame Street character who is sitting at a restaurant complaining about the fly in his soup. He had the messiest matted down brown hair all over the back of his head.

Oddly enough, just like his Muppet counterpart, he had bushy eyebrows, a big pink button nose and a giant bald spot on the top of his head. And if all THAT wasn't bad enough, he had white goggle marks around his eyes as if he might have fallen asleep in a tanning bed.

I know it's sad that all I can come up with for analogies are Sesame Street characters but after all the years of having to watch Sesame Street with the kids, they are embedded in my psyche forever.

Looking at Ed, I was expecting Grover to come over at any minute to take his order. I was sitting there waiting for him to order soup so that I could watch a fly drop into it. He must have had great radar because he seemed to immediately know which one of us was Trish.

Maybe Janie was pointing at Trish behind her back or maybe it was the new push up bra Trish was wearing that made her boobs say "Come and get me baby." Whatever the reason, Ed was all over it. He pulled up a chair right next to her and parked his ugly ass down as if to say, "Here I am honey, the man of your dreams." He held out his hand to Trish and attempting to avoid the cooties, she barely skimmed it as he introduced himself.

I watched a tiny stream of spit detonate out of his mouth and land above her left breast. Judging by the look on her face, I know she saw it too. Trish looked as if she had just stepped in a pile of dog shit and couldn't get it off of her shoe. The other two guys introduced themselves to us while Janie kept insisting to anyone who would listen, "Oh isn't Ed the sweetest, nicest guy you've ever met?"

A minute later, Trish jumped up so fast that she almost fell over on top of me. She sprinted to the bathroom and I was right behind her. Even walking as fast as I could, I think I got there a full five minutes after she did. It looked as if she was trying to run right out of her own skin. I walked into the bathroom unsure of how to console her.

When I got there I found her up against the wall crying her

eyes out. "What a disaster this is." I said to her. She looked at me, mascara running down her face, saying, "Oh my god, I can't do this! Is this what I'm in for? I never thought it was going to be like this! I can't believe she thinks I would be interested in *that*."

I tried my best to comfort my friend but I knew she was right. The whole thing had to be devastating. I reassured her that indeed that guy was not even close to being in her league and that she could have any guy she wanted—Especially with those boobs. I explained to her that Janie could be a bit flighty at times but that she really was trying to help and had good intentions.

We went back to the bar and told Janie that we needed to leave. We had all had enough of this awkward, unexpected blind date set-up and none of us had even ordered dinner yet. I think we knocked over a few customers in our haste to get out of there.

All I remember is Janie yelling behind us desperately trying to get us to come over to her house. She was screaming, "But I have a bar down in my basement! I have Rum! I have food! C'mon, I'll give you, whatever you want! Hey, I even have a box of Webkinz for your kids!" Now I had heard it all. Janie was trying to bribe us with...stuffed animals? Apparently, she had overstocked the boutique she owned and had a few extra Webkinz to spare. She would stop at nothing in order to get "Mr. Nice Guy" laid.

Most of us had lost our appetite but we decided to go to a Chinese place down the street. We were so relieved to finally eat dinner, relax and rehash the nightmare of an evening we had suffered. None of us could quite believe our ears when we heard a woman at the bar talking about sex toys. It was too much of a coincidence to be real.

We all looked at Mo inquisitively. It turned out that the woman boldly talking about sex toys was pushing her very own products!

Yup, she was in fact, nothing less than a sex toy sales rep and just imagine our surprise when we found out she was hosting parties in our part of town. She brought over a stack of brochures to our table to see if we'd be interested in hosting some of our own.

We had so much fun flipping through the pages and showing Mo all of the things she'd never seen before. We were convinced it was a cosmic sign that she had to book a party and get all kinds of free stuff. We knew her husband would be thrilled.

Mo never did end up booking the party but nevertheless, she got quite an education that night. The more she gazed, the harder we laughed and the better we all felt after the blind date fiasco.

Eventually Trish realized that Janie was only trying to help in her own kooky way but the whole experience that night had really hit upon a raw nerve and felt like a big slap in the face.

Thankfully for Trish, a few months later she had a run in with the guy who was servicing her mother's pool and now he is servicing her. We call him "The Cabana Boy" and he is a long way from the man with the fly in his soup from Sesame Street.

Despite the road of hell Trish has traveled on, the rest of us married ladies have now found ourselves living vicariously through her. I mean, who wouldn't want to take a dip with a Cabana Boy every once in awhile? I'm sure that guy could give Janie's "purple passion" a run for her money any day of the week or time of night–whatever the case may be.

The point is that Trish found someone to make her happy. And she didn't even need Janie's help (or big box of Webkinz) to find him.

Percocet & Potpourri

MY FRIEND JANIE OWNS THE CUTEST LITTLE BOUTIQUE. She sells everything from candles to jewelry. Like pretty much every small business owner in a depressed economy, she has been struggling to keep her head above water and it hasn't been easy. People, especially in a crummy economy, generally stop buying items in an adorable downtown boutique.

While it's true that a Pandora bracelet may be considered one of those basic needs to some women, when things get rough and you have a family to feed, the boutique goes out the window and the grocery bill takes over.

In a vodka induced brain storming session, Janie came up with an award winning idea to help start the cash rolling in. She invited our friend Chrissy, who sells Silpada, to come into the boutique and host a joint sales event. She agreed to give Chrissy the entire counter to display all of her items. Each woman invited to the event would then invite as many additional people as they could, in the hope that they would be promoting each other's businesses.

Since it would be closed to the public, she was even more excited to announce that she would be serving cocktails. It sounded like a fantastic idea to me and I remember looking forward to that night for weeks before it finally arrived. Janie and Chrissy together are definitely a dynamic duo for sure and I was certain it would add up to be one incredibly, exciting night.

Too bad for me that I can't speak to how incredible or exciting that night actually was, considering I have no recollection of anything beyond my first glass of wine and handful of chips with mango salsa.

Never in my wildest dreams could I ever have imagined that night would take a downward plunge the way it did. The only small bit of good that came out of that party was the gorgeous ring and bracelet I must have bought while in a state of delirium. The drawback to that purchase would have to be that every time I wear either one of those items, I can't help but get a little bit queasy while remembering the HELL which I endured that night and into the next day.

The evening started out the same way all of my friend's other parties always do, with lots of laughs and lots of wine. All the women we knew loved the idea of shopping at Janie's boutique to buy not only all of the unique items she generally stocks but Chrissy's beautiful sterling silver jewelry as well. It was a great turnout and far more people showed up for the event than any of us would have expected.

As the party got underway, I was feeling pretty good. I actually felt better than I normally would have because I'd just had my hair done that afternoon. Seriously, how much can go wrong when you're having a good hair day? For me good hair days are few and far between and usually only happen when I've literally just stepped out of a salon. I am definitely esthetically challenged and can't do my own hair to save my life.

Before the party, I popped in to see my friend Sue, an esthetician at a salon next to Janie's boutique. Sue had also been invited to the shopping extravaganza that night, so she hadn't scheduled any of her clients for that afternoon.

We had some time before the party when I had stopped by to chat, and she wanted to do my makeup. She had been taking classes and was eager to practice the latest techniques she'd learned, so I said, "Sure, why not? It'll be fun!" It was almost a bit too good to be true, having both my hair *and* makeup professionally done all on the same day.

Usually my makeup routine consists of moisturizer, mascara and occasionally a once over with my favorite lipstick. That's about as extravagant as I get. I think Sue went a tad overboard when I said, "Do whatever you want."

I can still remember how stunned I was when she handed me a mirror and I saw the odious pink lipstick on my lips. It was as chalky and pink as Pepto Bismol. My eyelids were painted with a shimmery sapphire eye shadow and I looked as though I was ready to take center stage in a musical. I really didn't care, since I was the one who had offered up my face as her guinea pig. Judging from the way my face looked, she was gonna need a whole lot more practice. After the make-up overload, we headed next-door, eager for a good time.

My face turned out to be the least of my concerns that night. After a few sips of wine, I started to feel sweaty and my stomach began to cramp up. God knows I don't get out enough to let a little cramping send me home in a hurry. I wasn't going to let it get me down. Well, at least that was my plan, until the grip of death took over.

These were no ordinary run of the mill cramps; these were kick-your-ass-take-your-breath-away cramps. For all I knew, it could have been a cyst bursting, a kidney stone or appendicitis. Whatever "it" was, the result was causing excruciating pain. I usually don't even like to take aspirin for pain, however, these killer cramps were screaming for something heavy duty. I suffered in silence for a while and finally decided to ask Sue if she had anything for the pain. As she watched my pupils dilate, she said she had left her purse out in the back room of Janie's store but thought she might have some Motrin.

Sensing my desperation, she took off in a hurry. A few minutes later she returned with two white pills and assured me they would do the trick. I stupidly made the assumption that she was handing me Motrin and as I washed them down with the rest of my wine, I never gave it a second thought.

For about the next ten to fifteen minutes after taking the pills, the pain was gone. I felt wonderful, euphoric and ecstatic. At that point, I probably should have realized that it wasn't normal to feel such bliss simply from a couple of Motrin. I felt invincible and was really flying high, which was why I had such trouble while deciding whether to buy the ring or the bracelet. I vaguely remember saying, "Why not? I'll buy them both!" And I did.

I was on top of the world showing off my new jewelry. All the while, I was still wearing the Pepto Bismol on my lips. Then, right in the middle of a conversation with Chrissy's mom, I boarded the imaginary teacups. Round and round I went, spinning out of control, while a haze began to settle all around my head. I felt so strangely that I couldn't focus on anything. Before the conversation was even over, everything suddenly went black.

When Chrissy called me the next morning to check up on me,

I had the misfortune of hearing her tell me everything, in great detail that had happened the rest of that night. Apparently, not only did I walk out into the middle of traffic to head to another bar, once inside, I ran into my friend Dee from high school and blatantly told her off.

I guess in my crazed state of mind, I was angry at Dee for being in town and not calling me. Little did I know she had left several voicemails on my cell phone. Unfortunately, I was in no way capable of answering a call from her, or from anyone for that matter. All she said when she saw me was, "Hello there", while I responded with every profanity I could muster up.

After those pleasantries, I downed a raspberry martini before Chrissy dragged me out to her minivan, where I proceeded to throw up all over the floor and dashboard on the ride home. She also informed me that I threw up all over my own driveway and warned me that I might have a few bruises on my ass from falling (more than once), along the way when I walked into my house. She was so confused and couldn't figure out what had happened to me.

Between the purchase of the bracelet and ring, to the moments of sheer madness that unfolded immediately afterward, she had never seen me so out of control. She kept asking me, "Exactly how much wine *did* you have last night? I told her it was after I took the "Motrin" I remembered I had started to feel woozy... THAT was when we started to piece it all together.

She asked who had given me the pills and if I was absolutely positive they were actually Motrin. I told her I had gotten the pills from Sue, who is practically saintly enough to be canonized. The whole situation made no sense to either of us. Chrissy called her mother-in-law, who is a nurse, and asked her if mixing Motrin and wine together could produce the kind of side effects

I experienced. Of course the answer was a moot point because it all depended on the quantity of wine (never mind the raspberry martini), and obviously, I had no idea how much wine I actually drank the night before.

Chrissy said I should call Sue and ask her if she was sure it was actually Motrin she'd given me. I figured it couldn't hurt, so I gave her a quick call. Sue told me she had gotten the pills from Janie, she had assumed they were Motrin, because that's what she'd asked for. Sue told me that I should probably call Janie and ask her about the pills. The plot thickened.

I gave Janie a call and asked her what it was exactly she'd given Sue to give me for my cramps the night before. She immediately said, "Oh my god! She was asking for you? I had no idea! I thought Sue was asking for herself. I gave her Percocet—It's the strongest pain medication I have in my arsenal. Every so often, Sue gets that raking back pain like I get, and if she forgets to bring her medication, I give her a couple of Percocet and it works like a charm. I didn't worry about giving her the pills because she's never had any side effects when I've given it to her in the past. You aren't supposed to mix that shit with alcohol but I knew Sue wasn't drinking last night. I *never* would have given you any because I knew you had already been sipping the wine."

Talk about confusion and miscommunication! I wondered why Sue hadn't just told Janie the pills were for me? I guess it didn't seem like such a big deal to her at the time. After all, she was only trying to help a friend in need, right?

For me though, it was a big deal. A *very* big deal. Even after all of this time, I still can't quite believe the havoc it wreaked on me. I have never been so sick in my life. Unless I count my twenty-first birthday, which was the night I drank seven Alabama Slammas that left me hung-over and bed ridden for two whole days.

I felt two inches tall when Chrissy told me I had puked in her minivan. I was completely horrified that I had done such a thing and what was worse, I couldn't remember even having done it. Chrissy and I both had sons playing in a baseball game that agonizing morning after. Since I was chained to the toilet bowl, I missed the game.

Chrissy's husband made it a point to tattletale to MY husband by telling him how drunk I'd gotten at the party and spared no details about what I did to—or rather *in*—his wife's minivan when she'd given me a ride home. It was all so utterly degrading and I was beyond ashamed. Of course, neither Chrissy's husband, nor mine, knew anything about the Percocets.

When I called Sue back and told her what had happened to me, she felt just terrible about the whole thing. She was profusely apologetic and she said she would never make that mistake again.

I shudder at the memory of my husband telling me to go outside and hose off the bright purple puke all over our driveway. He didn't believe a word of my "accidental drug" explanation and had no sympathy for me. None. He and Chrissy's husband both had an absolute field day at my expense. For weeks they made all kinds of terrible jokes, all the while berating me about that regrettable night.

As if that wasn't bad enough, I felt even worse when I thought about Chrissy cleaning all of my purple puke out of her minivan in her own driveway. Picturing her doing that, I knew she was suffering right there along with me and that wasn't fair. Not at all.

When I eventually felt better, I went out and bought Chrissy anything I could find with a wonderful smell. I suppose I thought it just might help take the stink of my puke out of her minivan as well as her mind. I discovered, in my search for all things aromatic, that I love the smell of Pomegranate. It has a sweet-smelling, fresh and fragrant bouquet for the nose. And it was exactly what I was looking for!

I'll admit that I did go a little bit overboard with the Pomegranate. I bought pomegranate-scented candles, air fresheners, essential oils and potpourri. I bought absolutely everything I could get my hands on to try to make up for all of the trouble I had caused her.

If I'd been able to give Chrissy a new minivan, I would have. I couldn't have felt more like a piece of crap if I'd tried. She was completely forgiving and understanding, as I would have been if *she* had been the one puking in my car, because it's what best friends will do for each other. And this is just one more example of why we need our best friends.

If we left it up to our husbands for understanding and support, we would be thrown to the dogs. No forgiveness, no understanding, no sympathy and absolutely no excuses. Certainly no pomegranate scented potpourri.

But, you might be able to score a stern look while being told to, "Just get out there with the damn hose and clean it up!"

Women & Wine

ONCE YOU BECOME A MOM, there isn't a lot of time for socializing. I remember before I had children, I could actually go to the mall with my girlfriends AND go out to lunch *on the same day.*

A couple of kids later, it's hard to remember the last time I was at a mall, let alone out to lunch with a girlfriend. I just know it doesn't happen very often.

Come to think of it, I probably couldn't tell you the last time I went to the bathroom by myself, or at least without some little person barging through the door catching me midstream.

I know that I am not the only mother in the world who has felt isolated or trapped under several piles of dirty laundry and a sink full of dishes. After all, aren't these the reasons mothers long ago dreamed up the idea of selling Tupperware?

In my opinion, the Tupperware movement is right up there with burning bras. I know it may be a far stretch, equating women's liberation with the freedom to store food securely in plastic containers, but let's face facts; it was never *really* about food storage. It was all about women and wine. I know this because if it was really about the Tupperware, they would have come up with a better way for the covers to stay on and not mysteriously disappear into the land of the lost lids.

Tupperware may be what first launched us all into the home party phenomenon but we've definitely had quite an interesting journey over the past few decades.

It may be true that all the wine drinking has sparked a lot of creativity on our part or maybe it's just the natural process of evolution. Either way, I am grateful for the progress. Thankfully, we have learned to think outside of the container and moved on to much more exciting possibilities.

Although Tastefully Simple and Pampered Chef can be fun parties, the purchases we make do require work on our part. Oh sure, the dips are amazing but everyone knows that they don't prepare themselves. That Pampered Chef chopper I bought last year is great but it still takes my hands to actually pump it up and down before the onions are as small as I want them to be. Not to mention I have to pull the entire gadget apart to clean it out properly when I'm finished.

Speaking of pumping and gadgets, I almost forgot about the infamous Sex Toy parties. Now, I'm sure the Sex Toy parties are up for debate as to whether or not the products should be categorized as "work". However, I would like to throw in my two cents since, after all, it is my story and I say that anything requiring me to stay up past my kids' bedtime is work. Besides, the only thing I ever dared to buy at those parties was the penis shaped ice cubes. Close friends or not, how many women would really feel comfortable buying sex toys in front of an audience?

I remember how embarrassing it was when the hostess of one such sex toy party passed something with rabbit ears around the circle of women in attendance, I thought I would die on the spot as it sat there quietly buzzing in my hand. I swear it was worse than a game of hot potato. Just thinking about it now, I can feel my palms starting to sweat so let's move on to the "Naughty Nightie" parties.

Maybe a more fitting name for them would be the Naughty Nightmare parties. After a few drinks, we suddenly find ourselves actually believing the hostess when she says, "You will look amazing in that, you'd never know in a million years that you've had two kids." All giddy from the wine we reply, "Are you serious? Well, in that case, I'll take one in every color!" Too bad when the wine wears off and we actually try them on at home, the mirror is much more truthful than the hostess.

As with every situation, you gotta weigh the pros and the cons. The "pro" with the naughty nighties is definitely that our husbands never complain about the spending we've done when we walk in with all those sexy nighties. One of the "cons" with the naughty nighties is that when we realize that once we've bought the damn things, we actually have to wear them. Not to mention that when we wear them we'll be forced to shave our legs, which again, would be work bordering on torture.

Since all of these party items really didn't seem to be worth their weight in wine, it was time yet again to come up with something new.

We charged forward with a mission of finding something to buy and sell in the comfort of our friend's homes that didn't require us to do any actual work. So out with the Tupperware, the Naughty Nighties, the cookware, dips and vibrating bunnies and on to the vast array of...sterling silver jewelry!

Seriously though, no matter what it may be that is bought or sold, it's all nothing more than a gigantic excuse to consume large quantities of wine with other moms who are trying to numb the pain of their day to day drudgery.

The first jewelry party I attended was at my friend Jenn's house many years ago when my kids were both in elementary school. I can remember the pure joy and delight I experienced immediately upon walking into her kitchen. What a beautiful sight it was for my frazzled and exhausted eyes! I wanted to revel in the moment and take in all of the deep, rich and dazzling colors. Oh God, how they all shined and sparkled! What a wonderful assortment of treasures displayed all along the counter. There were so many choices, each one a little more enticing than the next. I didn't even know where to start.

All this indecision and I hadn't even *entered* the room with the jewelry yet, I was talking about the wine. There was the Merlot, which was sweet yet full bodied, with a hint of cherry. The Chardonnay with subtle traces of peach and white grape, not to mention the home made Sangria garnished with fresh slices of fruit.

As if choosing my very own flavor of wine wasn't exciting enough, I was also able to choose my own glass! There they were, beautiful vessels displayed on the counter so eloquently. Shiny crystal in all sizes shapes and designs perfect to complement any libation.

Choices, choices, choices! Everywhere I turned there were more things for me to choose. This never happened at home.

Sure I might choose which load of laundry to do first, colored or whites? I could choose whether I should load the dishwasher first or scrub the bathrooms. But those weren't fun and exciting choices.

Suddenly, I felt so sophisticated and almost worldly. My adorable friend Jenn, the hostess, even had little charms to go on the bottom of the wine glasses so we wouldn't get confused about which glass belonged to which woman.

I had never seen these little wine glass charms before and I was quite impressed. Granted, I don't get out much but still, what a great idea! Little charms to put on your wine glass! Will wonders never cease?

I buckled down to make my choices. First, I chose the Merlot, then I chose a tall, wide, crystal wine glass and finally I chose the cute little "flip-flop" charm to put on my glass.

When no one was looking, I felt the need to pinch myself because for a moment, I really did think I was dreaming. First of all, just the fact that I was able to go to this party with no kids attached to my hip was a luxury by itself. Add to that I was shopping for beautiful jewelry, while engaging in real live adult conversation and top it all off with large quantities of wine? Well, it doesn't take a mathematical genius to figure out that the sum equaled my Heaven.

I'd really never enjoyed shopping for jewelry before. I think it's mostly because of the uncomfortable stuffy feeling I get as soon as I walk in the door. Unless of course it's Janie's boutique, where none of the ordinary rules apply. If you are a good friend of Janie's, she will gladly take you out back to her private room and pour you a glass of wine before you shop.

Then again, I can't really fault all the other store owners for abiding by the liquor laws and not offering alcohol to their customers. Maybe I'm on to something here! It really wouldn't be a bad idea for the big jewelers to think about applying for a liquor license. I'll bet if they started offering cocktails at jewelry stores they would see a huge increase in the profits. Can you imagine how much bigger our engagement rings would be if our husbands were given a few Sam Adams while shopping for them?

I loved the way the sales representative at the jewelry party had set up the display table. I have to give her a lot of credit, because it really looked fabulous. A gorgeous black velvet cloth was draped ever so glamorously over the dining room table and everywhere I looked I could see sparkling silver. What a smart idea to use the black velvet! It added a touch of class and at the same time, was very forgiving of all the wine spills.

I wasn't even on my second glass of wine before I knocked one over on the table. I was intrigued by how the velvet just soaked it right up and never even left a mark.

Everything was so pretty against the dark black–the earrings, bracelets, necklaces and even rings all seemed to shine so brightly. Who would have thought there would be so many things to shop for right there in Jenn's home?

It's really never a good idea to shop while under the influence. If husbands were smart they would advocate for an SWUI law to go into effect. Granted, it's highly unlikely that you would actually kill somebody while shopping under the influence. Unless of course you are in Boston at Filene's semiannual Bridal Gown Sale, which is dangerous enough *without* booze. Add alcohol to a thousand ruthless, bargain-hunting brides-to-be and I assure you, somebody's gonna get hurt, or maimed, if not killed.

This is the reason that the Bridal Gown Sale event is always planned for the wee hours of the morning. It goes on so early that I seriously doubt if those women have even gotten in their second cup of coffee yet, and it's a good thing because the adrenaline alone is enough to hype them up.

I personally have never had the experience of such an event due to my chronic shopping anxiety but I have had plenty of friends who have. Shopping war stories are part of the reason I am so grateful someone came up with the idea of shopping in friends' homes while drinking wine. It definitely takes the edge off. It's not spending the money that makes me nervous, it is the crowds of people. Many who are *serious* shoppers. At least when I'm shopping at a friends' home, it's so much more relaxed and I can breathe.

My husband actually loves my shopping anxiety because it saves him a ton of money. I think that's probably half the reason he married me. Even he gets bothered by my shopping anxiety at times, though, like that one Thanksgiving when we went to the grocery store and he had to get me out of there before we got the Turkey. Crazy people everywhere–running around stuffing their carts with turkey basters, big aluminum pans, cranberry sauce and pumpkin pie filling. "Get me out of here right now!" I demanded. My hands were shaking as I broke out in a cold sweat. I realize this isn't normal but I have absolutely no control over it.

Since I can trace back to the exact moment the phobia started, I guess it technically falls into the category of PTSD. My younger sister and I begged my mom to let us go shopping alone one day soon after I had turned twelve. She agreed and gave us our first taste of freedom. Let's just say I didn't fare too well. She no sooner left, when I had an all out panic attack thinking she was going to forget to come back and get us. I ended up in the restrooms throwing up. To this day the fear stays with me and no matter what I do, I can't shake it. The minute I enter a store, it kicks in. So on that note, I can honestly say that shopping in small groups with trusted friends, while drinking wine is a perfect solution for someone with my issues.

I've been to so many of these jewelry parties by now that I think I own everything in all of the catalogues. I've hosted my own jewelry party, all of my friends have hosted parties and one of them even decided to sell it for a while.

The thing is, if you're going to attempt to sell it, you really do have to have a talent for sales–otherwise you're gonna fail. My friend sucked at it, because not only would she tell people that they didn't have to buy anything but she would practically offer to buy it for them. Needless to say, she wasn't able to continue selling it for very long.

Sooner or later, you do run out of people who are willing to host these parties, because every single one of their friends have already hosted parties and the friends of their friends have done the same. Our fridges may not be stocked with food but I can guarantee you this, our jewelry boxes are spilling over with sterling silver.

Sometime between the hangover and the credit card statement, you realize that not only couldn't you afford all of this dazzling jewelry, but also since you have no life, when will you ever have an occasion to wear it all? Oh sure, you can wow the receptionist at your kids pediatrician's office with your blue topaz ring and I'm sure the stock boy in the produce department at your local grocery store will gaze admiringly at your hammered sterling earrings. You might even get an appreciating glance from your kid's teacher at the next parent/teacher conference.

Other than these mediocre hopes and dreams, there probably won't be many occasions to actually wear your beautiful silver jewelry. I guess it doesn't really matter because when it all comes down to it, we really do know that the sterling silver is a hell of a lot prettier than plastic containers with no lids. Plus it doesn't require us to do any real work.

And in the end, it truly is all about the women and the wine. *Especially* if there are going to be cute little charms for wine glasses involved.

The Sisterhood of the Absolut

EVERY SO OFTEN YOU GOTTA BREAK OUT OF THE MOMMY SHACKLES, kick off the ball and chain and let loose. I love "mom's night out". This is when we all get to dig deep and resurrect the happy, carefree girls we used to be. While the Calgon commercial promises a similar escape, it's obvious that the lady lavishing up her silky smooth skin with cashmere bubbles doesn't have kids.

Nothing would plummet Calgon sales more than a couple of tyrants barging into the bathroom yelling, "Mom, she punched me!" "Yeah but Mom, he spit in my hair!" I don't remember the last time I took a bath, but I have done something far more stress relieving than a bath in my house could ever be.

In some kind of miraculous fashion, "the girls" and I scheduled an evening free of babies, husbands and laundry. We ditched our stretchy pants and our husband's sweatshirts that, somewhere along the line, had become our uniforms.

We started our evening by having dinner at a nearby restaurant downtown. We all knew the food would be mediocre at best but we sacrificed good food to be closer to home, because closer to home meant more time to spill our guts and drink our wine. Our conversation was in full flow (and so were the drinks), when the clock seemed to speed up. Seeing the time, and how late it was getting, we felt as though The Grim Reaper was suddenly coming to steal us away in order to draft us back into our realities.

That particular night, we decided we could outrun The Reaper and put off our realities a bit longer. We found ourselves careening into a Martini Bar down the street, a couple of doors down from the restaurant. My friend Chrissy was whining about having had to forgo dessert for the martinis.

In an effort to quiet her down, I suggested we compromise and try the Chocolate Martini. She said, "It sounds so amazing, but you *know* I always pass out when I drink vodka." Chrissy screamed as if she might have won the lottery when, once we sat down at the Martini Bar, the bartender whipped out a dessert menu. She settled on an absurdly large piece of double fudge cake with Oreos and a glass of chardonnay. In unison everyone else chimed in to order Chocolate Martinis.

I almost fell off my bar stool when our friend Mo agreed to try one. She's the "goody-goody" of our group and her drink of choice is usually club soda with a lime. Sometimes she'll splurge and order a splash of cranberry juice in it. Not on that particular "mommy's night out". On that particular night, Mo flashed the bartender a beaming, and out of character, smile while she provided an explanation for her sudden change of heart. She said, "I'm not really big on Vodka, but I AM a major chocoholic, so why not?"

We'd only finished about half of our Chocolate Martinis

when the lights flickered and the bartender yelled, "Drink 'em up people! C'mon! Let's go!" Listening to him give us the "last call" transported me right back to my early twenties. It had been almost two *decades* since I'd been thrown out of a bar and that sad fact was making me feel old—way too old.

Before I could wallow too deeply in my old lady sorrows, Janie blurted out, "Oh shit, are you fucking kidding me? It's last call already?" Seemingly unaware of her surroundings, her speech was a slurred mess and she was dropping F bombs like a trucker in a dingy diner. Janie is the self-professed "bad girl" in our group. She leaves nothing to the imagination and she has a great affinity for the F word, particularly when she's drinking and especially when she's drunk.

While Janie was uttering her expletives, Mo whipped her head around and shot her a look to kill. She said, "Jeez Janie, would you tone it down? You're out of control! Seriously, that's enough." Chrissy, ignoring Mo's commands piped up with her own brand of profanity.

Even though Chrissy generally wasn't one to use deprecating language in public, she was still a force to be reckoned with. Any woman who can successfully break up boxing matches between three young boys on a daily basis oughta be taken seriously in my book.

Chrissy commanded respect when she glared at the bartender and said, "You can flick those lights all you want Mister, but I'll be *damned* if you're gonna ruin our good time." Janie retorted, "That's right girl! You fucking tell him! We don't need this high class bar—let's go to my place." Janie threw her head back and laughed so hard I thought her neck was gonna snap. I imagined her head rolling to the floor thinking that even if her head had actually detached, somehow the F words would still be flying out.

With that, Mo shoved her bar stool back, grabbed her purse, and stormed off to the ladies room. She probably hadn't even flushed the toilet before we were out the door and running down the street to Janie's.

Chrissy chased after us pleading, "You can't just leave her in there like that! What is the matter with you guys? It's flat out rude!" We kept right on running ignoring her pleas. Chrissy is the queen of etiquette, so she refused to follow us and instead, ventured back inside and nobly waited for Mo. We were elated to take Janie up on the invite to her place because by "place" she didn't mean her *actual* home where her nosey husband would surely be keeping a watchful eye on us.

Janie's boutique was only a few blocks up away from the bar, which meant it was close by and easily accessible. More importantly to all of us, for our purposes that evening, was that Janie always keeps a stash of booze in the back room of her boutique.

We all felt deviously sneaky to be at her store, in the dark and after hours. It was exhilarating when Janie unlocked the back door and we all followed her inside. Janie, being the only one of us who could properly open a bottle of wine, popped the cork and poured us all a glass. Moments later Chrissy and Mo, completely out of breath, stumbled through the back door.

We sat cross-legged in a circle on the storeroom floor of Janie's boutique. We devoured gossip, bottles of wine and an entire tub of cheese balls. If anyone noticed how stale the cheese balls were, they didn't utter a peep. Chrissy then enraptured us with a story about her youngest son, who threw his brother's brand new hundred dollar sneakers into the toilet bowl and peed on them.

Trying to picture Chrissy as she plucked urine filled sneakers out of the toilet had us in stitches because she's so squeamish over stuff like that. Janie was relentless with her interruptions and her F words, as she pouted while whimpering, "Poor fucking kid, I'll bet he never wears those sneakers again." Chrissy finally snapped at her, "Shut up Janie, you should be more worried about poor fucking ME!" That was a first. Chrissy usually *never* says a swear word without spelling it. I was impressed.

After Chrissy's irregular choice of vocabulary, Mo abruptly stood up and I figured she was outta there, until I saw her hands shoot up into the air. It seemed the Chocolate Martini hit her all at once and she suddenly stumbled into the counter, knocking over a jewelry display as she did. I was surprised to see her moving in the opposite direction of the door.

Instead of leaving our new hotbed of debauchery, Mo fumbled through her purse and pulled out a disc. She then headed for the back wall and asked Janie where she kept the CD player. I cringed with fearful anticipation and wondered whether we would be subjected to classical or jazz. She popped in her CD, hit "play", jumped up on the counter and started dancing.

We all watched with awe while she started swaying her hips back and forth singing about Piña Coladas. Before she got to the part about making love at midnight, she fell off the counter and hit the floor—hard—but she got right back up on her feet and without missing a beat, she proudly announced, "It's time for the martini confessions ladies! I'll go first! Wanna know what I despise more than anything?" she said with a slur. We all shook our heads in bewilderment, but before we could guess, she curled her lips up, squeezed her eyes shut like she just swallowed vinegar, and said, "Blow jobs."

In a split second, my opinion of "Miss Goody-Goody" drastically changed. She was definitely a far cry from the lady I thought she'd been all the years I'd known her. If one Chocolate Martini was all it took to transform her from Mary Poppins into Catwoman, I would personally make it my mission to make sure she had one in front of her whenever we went out.

In that instant, Mo "Goody Goody" had accomplished the unimaginable. For the first time, probably ever, someone was actually holding her own against Janie! And the fact that Mo was the one to do it? Before that night, the idea of Mo and Janie toe to toe was even more unthinkable. She kept replaying the Piña Colada song until finally she said, "Come on, whose next? Someone else has to confess something."

I disclosed my own confession by saying, "Okay, I'll go next. Well, I was three months pregnant when I got married." As Jenn took a big gulp of wine, she said dismissively, "Oh, I can beat that! If you look closely at *my* wedding photos, you'll see my oldest son is in them."

"Oh big deal you guys! Man up, would you? I bring vodka in Poland Spring bottles to all the little league games." Janie confessed with a smirk. Chrissy then admitted, "I have a crush on my Vet, and I pray for my cat to get sick, just so I can make a visit." With my curiosity piqued, I immediately had to know who her Vet was. As soon as she said, "Dr. P." I jumped up with a shriek! I too, had been harboring a secret crush on him for years. Until our "Martini Confessions", we didn't even know we used the same Vet! Go figure.

It was Mo's turn again and she divulged that one night her

oldest son had caught her having sex with her husband. Janie declared, "Better to get caught having sex with your husband, than to get caught having sex with someone *else's* husband." Mo added, "Well, we yanked the blankets up over us as fast as we could, but he was already standing over us and staring in horror. He was crying and said he heard loud monsters breathing and he mimicked the noises, with big loud huffing sounds. I told him that the washing machine belt broke and that was what all the scary noise was about."

After Mo told us about scarring her son for life, she then motioned to a top shelf where she could see a big bottle of Absolut and said, "This is just like that movie where those girls share stories and pass around an old pair of jeans! Except we're passing around Vodka, right Janie?" Janie didn't think twice before she vaulted up off the floor and graciously obliged.

While she was pouring shots all around she drunkenly declared, "We are the sisterhood of the traveling vodka!" I was stunned when I saw Chrissy throw one down because I figured she would pass out shortly thereafter. She surprised me when, on that magical night, she stepped up and did her part for the sisterhood.

Only one of us in the circle had remained mum all throughout our "Martini Confessions", and that was Kelly. Janie said, "You'd better start fucking confessing something young lady, or we're gonna kick you out of the sisterhood!" Hesitantly Kelly murmured, "Um...Okay, okay, I got one. Hearing the Piña Colada song reminded me of last summer when my sister and I got shit faced on Piña Colada's and did something we shouldn't have. You guys better swear to secrecy or I'm not divulging anything!" Mo yelled, "Yessss! Bring it on! Oooooh *now* it's getting good!"

We fell silent and were stoically half expecting someone to whip out a bible for us to place our hands on. We were ready to take an oath to the sisterhood.

When I really thought about the way all of us were *so* eager to drink in Kelly's dirty little secret, the whole thing seemed kind of pathetic. As she began spilling it, we felt as though we were instantly transformed into kids huddled around a campfire, entranced while listening to a ghost story. When had our lives become *this* mundane?

We were all captivated as we listened to her tell us how one night the previous summer, she had gotten really discouraged with her husband Greg (who was a recovering alcoholic), when she found out he had started drinking again. She decided to drag her little sister to Newburyport for some good old-fashioned soul searching. They sat on a pier overlooking the harbor while drinking Piña Coladas.

Kelly told us it was the first time she had actually seriously contemplated divorcing her husband. She wasn't sure how she would take her beloved boys away from their dad, at the same time, she was afraid that keeping them exposed to his drinking was worse than the unknown.

Kelly and her sister had spent every summer on the ocean when they were growing up but hadn't been on a boat in years. She said that nostalgia spread over her as she watched the boats docking in the harbor and after she had one or two more drinks, she proclaimed, "I'm gonna get us a boat ride." Her sister didn't think much about what Kelly had said until she looked up and saw her making a bee line toward an over sized white boat–two guys on board.

She imparted that her sister had tried to intervene before it was too late. Her sister had tried to save her but was held up by some psycho woman on the docks. Apparently the crazy lady was shouting at Kelly's sister, relentlessly demanding to know if she would accept Jesus as her one true Savior. She was reading from a pamphlet while yelling, "Do you want to go to Heaven or do you want to go to Hell?" Kelly's sister was petrified standing on the docks, watching this unhinged hag with her cascading mane of silver hair blowing in the wind. According to Kelly, the deranged woman had cratered skin, eyes as black as onyx and scared the wits right out of her poor sister.

Despite her fears, Kelly's sister mustered the nerve to yell back at the crone, "Hey listen lady, my sister is about to go to Hell down there on that boat and it's more important for me to save her *ass* right now than to save my soul." After that, she was off and running down the dock to rescue Kelly.

Poor Kelly began to bite nervously at one of her fingernail's when she confessed, "By the time, my baby sister got down to the boat, I was already lip locked with the captain. He couldn't have been a day over thirty and had the most piercing blue eyes God ever created. Boy, I was about to get myself into some serious trouble! That is, until my sister jumped on board more menacing than a wild tiger. I don't know if she was more pissed off or jealous, but believe me, it didn't help the situation when she saw how butt ugly the other guy was. He was downright scary. He looked like a worn out old surfer dude with scraggly blond hair and bloodshot eyes. He reeked of fish guts and Budweiser. I wish you could have seen her face when he handed her a can of beer out of a plastic grocery bag! But just in the nick of time, thunder crackled as a massive lightening bolt illuminated the sky right above us. It was as if that demon woman from the docks was sending us a sign to get the hell out of there. We ran for our lives and never looked back."

Kelly woke up the next morning to find both a business card and her wedding rings in her pocket. She felt guilty that she had taken off her wedding rings and had no idea how that business card had materialized into her possession.

Her recall of that night was fuzzy at best, but she remembered with complete certainty, whose card it was that she had pulled out of her pocket. The name on the card was unfamiliar but the company name underneath filled Kelly with a sudden sense of panic. She instantly recognized the small company name as the very same place where her husband Greg worked. It was such a small office that Kelly knew, beyond the shadow of a doubt, that the two men must have crossed paths on a daily basis.

Greg had been sober for several months following that regrettable night, when they had fought so bitterly, and their marriage had greatly improved as a result. She admitted to us that, although she and Greg were doing much better now that he was sober, she would never be stupid enough to confess her slip up to him. Although, after the business card discovery she decided it was necessary to avoid all company outings and holiday parties like the plague.

Kelly's was the last of the "Martini Confessions" that night, but we all left the back room of Janie's boutique knowing our "Girl's Night Out" was forever changed. After that night, it wasn't just about a bunch of mommies escaping for an evening "off duty", while trying to get our groove back. Our relationships with each other had evolved into a deeper connection than our children's friendships had forged for us.

On that magical night, we became something more than

a female equivalent of "drinking buddies". We had become a true sisterhood, deeper than any we could possibly have imagined when we first came together during that initial preschool playdate.

As our children have grown from toddlers to teens, we've nourished one another through it all—the joys, sorrows, laughter and tears. A lot has changed since our first night of "Martini Confessions" and our sisterhood has stood the test of time.

Throughout all of our travels and travails, together we have all agreed that sharing Absolut has been a lot more exciting than sharing an old pair of jeans.